# Edward D. Andrews

# THE EGYPTIAN EMPIRE
## Its Role in Biblical History

# THE EGYPTIAN EMPIRE

## Its Role in Biblical History

Edward D. Andrews

Christian Publishing House
Cambridge, Ohio

Copyright © 2025 Edward D. Andrews

All rights reserved. Except for brief quotations in articles, other publications, book reviews, and blogs, no part of this book may be reproduced in any manner without prior written permission from the publishers. For information, write, support@christianpublishers.org

*THE EGYPTIAN EMPIRE: Its Role in Biblical History* by Edward D. Andrews

ISBN-13: **9798281631440**

# Table of Contents

Preface ............................................................................. 7

INTRODUCTION ........................................................... 9

CHAPTER 1 How Did Egypt Shape Biblical History from the Time of Abraham to the Days of Jeremiah? ........................ 12

CHAPTER 2 How Did the Boundaries and Geography of Egypt Influence Its Role in Biblical History? ............................ 14

CHAPTER 3 How Did the Nile Shape Egypt's Economy and Its Role in Biblical History? ............................................... 19

CHAPTER 4 What Were the Principal Products of Egypt, and How Did They Shape Its Role in Biblical History? .......... 24

CHAPTER 5 Who Were the People of Egypt in Biblical Times? ................................................................................ 30

CHAPTER 6 What Do We Know About the Language of the Egyptians in Biblical Times? ............................................... 35

What Was the Nature of Egyptian Religion in Biblical Times? ................................................................................ 40

CHAPTER 7 How Did Animal Worship Reflect the Degrading Idolatry of Egypt? .................................................. 46

CHAPTER 8 Why Did Moses Insist That Israel's Sacrifices Would Be "Detestable to the Egyptians"? ............................. 51

CHAPTER 9 What Spiritual and Moral Qualities Were Lacking in Egyptian Religion? ............................................... 56

CHAPTER 10 What Were the Egyptian Beliefs About the Dead, and How Did They Contrast with Biblical Truth? ......... 61

CHAPTER 11 What Was Egyptian Life and Culture Like in the Biblical Period? ................................................................ 66

CHAPTER 12 What Does the Bible Reveal About Abraham's Visit to Egypt? ...................................................... 72

CHAPTER 13 What Role Did Joseph Play in Egypt, and How Did His Rise Demonstrate Jehovah's Sovereign Purpose? ............................................................................. 79

CHAPTER 14 What Is the Historical Significance of the Hyksos Period, and How Does It Relate to the Biblical Account of Joseph and Israel in Egypt? ................................................. 84

CHAPTER 15 What Does the Bible Reveal About Israel's Slavery in Egypt? ................................................................. 90

CHAPTER 16 What Role Did Egypt Play After Israel's Conquest of Canaan? ................................................................. 95

CHAPTER 17 How Did Egypt Respond to the Assyrian Invasion and What Was Its Role in Israel's History During This Period? ................................................................. 100

CHAPTER 18 How Did Egypt Suffer Defeat by Nebuchadnezzar, and What Was Its Role in the Fall of Judah? ................................................................. 105

CHAPTER 19 What Was Egypt's Role and Condition Under Persian Domination, and How Does This Fulfill Biblical Prophecy? ................................................................. 110

CHAPTER 20 What Was Egypt's Role and Condition Under Greek Rule, and How Did This Fulfill Biblical Patterns of Judgment? ................................................................. 115

CHAPTER 21 What Was Egypt's Condition Under Roman Rule, and How Did This Complete the Biblical Pattern of Judgment? ................................................................. 120

CHAPTER 22 What Do the Valuable Papyrus Finds Reveal About Egypt's History and the Reliability of the Biblical Record? ................................................................. 125

CHAPTER 23 What Do the Valuable Papyrus Finds from Egypt Reveal About Biblical Transmission and Historical Reliability? ................................................................. 131

CHAPTER 24 Summary and Theological Reflections on Egypt's Role in Biblical History ................................................................. 136

Bibliography ................................................................. 141

# Preface

The history of Egypt, one of the oldest and most formidable empires of the ancient world, intersects with the biblical record at multiple critical junctures, shaping the lives and destinies of Jehovah's covenant people. Yet despite Egypt's prominence in both secular and sacred history, modern treatments of its role in Scripture too often succumb to speculative theories, Higher Criticism, or allegorical reinterpretations that obscure the literal truth of the inspired Word. This work seeks to correct that trend by presenting a faithful, historically grounded study of Egypt as it appears in the Bible, honoring the integrity of the text as transmitted through the Spirit-guided apostles and prophets.

This book is written in defense of the historical accuracy of Scripture and in recognition of Jehovah's sovereign hand at work through the rise and fall of nations. Egypt's involvement with Israel—from the days of Abraham's sojourn to the oppressive regime of Pharaoh during the Exodus, from the Hyksos period and Joseph's exaltation to Egypt's political entanglements during the prophetic ministries of Isaiah and Jeremiah—serves as an unmistakable testimony to divine providence. The recurring appearance of Egypt across the biblical timeline is not accidental but purposeful, providing a backdrop for demonstrating Jehovah's justice, patience, and ultimate authority over human rulers.

Rejecting allegory, typology, and the errors of Critical Scholarship, this study adheres strictly to the historical-grammatical method of interpretation. The Scriptures are treated as the inerrant Word of God, accurately recording the events as they occurred within real historical contexts. Every effort has been made to avoid speculative interpretations, emotionalism, or mystical readings that distract from the plain meaning of the text. Instead, the biblical record is allowed to speak for itself, illuminated by archaeology, historical research, and linguistic study where such evidence supports the inspired testimony.

This work is not written merely as an academic exercise but as a contribution to the defense of biblical truth. Egypt is not portrayed here as a romanticized or enlightened culture, but as Scripture reveals it—a nation immersed in degrading idolatry, animal worship, and occult practices, standing at odds with the holiness of Jehovah. The moral bankruptcy of Egypt's religion, its deification of animals, and its priestly manipulation of magic contrast sharply with the ethical monotheism that Jehovah established through His covenant with Israel.

Throughout the chapters that follow, careful attention is given to the literal chronology of biblical events, including the Exodus in 1446 B.C.E., Israel's sojourn in Egypt beginning around 1876 B.C.E., and other datable milestones that connect the biblical text with the historical record. These dates are not conjecture but rest upon the solid foundation of scriptural testimony harmonized with trustworthy historical data.

It is my prayer that this book will aid readers in deepening their understanding of the biblical narrative, appreciating the historical reality of Egypt's empire without compromising doctrinal truth. May this work strengthen confidence in the Word of God, reminding us that all human power, however mighty, remains subject to the will of Jehovah, the true Sovereign of history.

*Edward D. Andrews*

Author of 220+ books and Chief Translator of he Updated American Standard Version (UASV)

# THE EGYPTIAN EMPIRE

# INTRODUCTION

Throughout the pages of sacred Scripture, Egypt occupies a place of profound significance, not as a footnote to biblical history, but as a recurring and formidable presence that shaped the course of Jehovah's dealings with His covenant people. Egypt emerges not only as a geographical neighbor to Israel but as a political force, a place of refuge, a land of oppression, and at times, an object of divine judgment. From the patriarchal era to the prophetic warnings that echoed at the close of Judah's monarchy, the Egyptian empire stands as a backdrop against which the sovereignty of Jehovah is consistently magnified.

This work does not seek to elevate Egypt as an enlightened culture or romanticize its civilization, as modern secular histories are often prone to do. Instead, it endeavors to explore Egypt's role within the biblical narrative on its own terms—examining the historical, cultural, geographical, and religious dimensions of Egypt as they intersect with the inspired record. The approach taken herein is grounded firmly in the historical-grammatical method of biblical interpretation, rejecting the distortions of allegory, typology, and speculative criticism. The purpose is not to find hidden meanings beneath the text, but to faithfully represent what the inspired writers recorded, allowing the Scripture itself to define Egypt's place in redemptive history.

The Egyptian empire's grandeur—its architectural achievements, military campaigns, agricultural abundance, and bureaucratic sophistication—did not shield it from the penetrating assessments of the biblical writers. The Egyptian gods, exalted by their worshipers and sustained by an intricate priestly system, were exposed as powerless before the might of Jehovah. Whether in the humiliation of Egypt's pantheon through the ten plagues of the Exodus, or in the repeated prophetic declarations of Egypt's downfall at the hands of rising empires such as Assyria, Babylon, and Persia, the message of Scripture remains consistent: Jehovah alone rules over nations and kings, raising them up and bringing them low according to His righteous will.

This book systematically examines the intersections between Egypt and biblical history across several key epochs. The early chapters address Egypt's influence during the patriarchal period—the journeys of Abraham, the rise of Joseph, and the eventual enslavement of Israel. Subsequent sections explore the geography and economy of Egypt, highlighting how its physical features, particularly the life-giving Nile, shaped its strength and stability. The religious practices of Egypt, including its notorious animal worship and occult superstitions, are analyzed in light of biblical revelation, exposing the moral and spiritual corruption at the heart of Egypt's religious system.

Special attention is given to the historical events surrounding the Exodus, the Hyksos period, and Egypt's later entanglements with Israel and Judah. The text also examines Egypt's interactions with world powers such as the Assyrians, Babylonians, Persians, Greeks, and Romans, showing how Egypt's decline fulfilled the prophetic warnings pronounced by Jehovah's spokesmen. The final chapters consider Egypt's legacy in biblical transmission, particularly through the papyri finds that provide valuable insight into historical reliability and textual preservation.

In approaching Egypt's history through the lens of Scripture, this study affirms the absolute trustworthiness of the biblical record. The dates, places, and events mentioned in the Bible are not mythological or symbolic but historical realities, firmly rooted in the flow of human history. The Egyptian empire, for all its grandeur and endurance, was but an instrument within Jehovah's broader purpose—the preservation of His people, the vindication of His holiness, and the unfolding of His plan of redemption for mankind.

Readers will find in the chapters that follow a consistent emphasis on Scripture as the supreme authority for interpreting historical events. Archaeology, linguistics, and historical research are employed not as substitutes for the Bible but as tools that confirm and clarify the inspired narrative. Where modern scholarship conflicts with Scripture, this work stands unapologetically with the biblical account, confident in the accuracy of the Word of God.

It is the author's hope that this study will deepen the reader's appreciation for the faithfulness of Jehovah across the centuries and provide a robust defense of the biblical portrayal of Egypt. More than a survey of history, this book seeks to contribute to the believer's understanding of how Jehovah accomplishes His purposes through nations and empires, ultimately demonstrating that no earthly power can thwart His sovereign will.

Edward D. Andrews

# CHAPTER 1 How Did Egypt Shape Biblical History from the Time of Abraham to the Days of Jeremiah?

**Introduction**

Throughout the entire biblical narrative, **Egypt** stands as one of the most frequently mentioned foreign powers, exerting profound influence upon the unfolding account of Jehovah's covenant people. From the earliest appearance of Egypt in the life of **Abraham**, through the **sojourn of Joseph** and the Israelites during the patriarchal period, to the dramatic events of the **Exodus under Moses,** and later in the era of **prophetic warning and judgment during Jeremiah's ministry**, Egypt serves not merely as a geopolitical neighbor but as a backdrop against which critical moments of divine revelation and historical fulfillment occur.

The prominence of Egypt in the Bible reflects its undeniable position as one of the most enduring and powerful civilizations of the ancient world. With its fertile Nile valley, monumental architecture, military prowess, and longstanding dynastic rule, Egypt possessed economic stability and cultural prestige that shaped the political environment of the ancient Near East for over two millennia. Yet in the pages of Scripture, Egypt represents more than an earthly empire; it symbolizes both a place of **refuge and oppression, opportunity and testing**, serving at various times as both protector and persecutor of the descendants of **Abraham**.

The biblical account treats Egypt as fully integrated into the covenantal history of Jehovah's dealings with humanity. Egypt's role is not peripheral but central, beginning with **Abraham's descent into Egypt due to famine** (Genesis 12:10), continuing through the rise of **Joseph to power under Pharaoh** (Genesis 41:41-46), extending through Israel's **four-century sojourn and enslavement**, climaxing in the **Exodus and the demonstration of Jehovah's power through the plagues,** and culminating in later prophetic episodes such as

# THE EGYPTIAN EMPIRE

**Jeremiah's confrontations with Egyptian political interference** during the late seventh and early sixth centuries B.C.E.

At each stage, Egypt's involvement with the people of Israel highlights crucial theological themes: the **testing of faith**, the **exposure of idolatry and human pride**, and the **vindication of Jehovah's sovereignty** over all nations. The Egyptian episodes provide tangible demonstrations of Jehovah's justice and mercy, often revealing both His longsuffering patience toward sinful nations and His uncompromising holiness that demands accountability.

This article will explore the multi-layered role of Egypt across four major biblical epochs:

- Egypt's interaction with **Abraham** as a sojourner.
- Egypt's elevation of **Joseph** to second in command, providing a temporary refuge and setting the stage for Israel's growth.
- Egypt's enslavement of Israel and the rise of **Moses**, leading to the climactic **Exodus**.
- Egypt's later role in the time of **Jeremiah**, including its attempts to influence or rescue Judah during the era of Babylonian ascendancy.

By tracing these historical periods and their scriptural contexts, this study will show how Egypt, though outside the line of promise, was used repeatedly by Jehovah to advance His purposes. The narrative will demonstrate that while Egypt often sought its own power and advantage, its very resistance to Jehovah became the means through which His **glory and dominion over the nations** were magnified.

From **Abraham's test of trust**, to **Joseph's rise as a deliverer**, to **Moses' confrontation with Pharaoh**, and finally to **Jeremiah's prophetic warnings**, Egypt's recurring presence in Israel's history underscores the reality that **no earthly power can thwart Jehovah's plans**. Whether as an oppressor or an occasional haven, Egypt's fate remains tied to the unfolding account of redemption, judgment, and divine sovereignty recorded in the inspired Word of God.

# CHAPTER 2 How Did the Boundaries and Geography of Egypt Influence Its Role in Biblical History?

**Boundaries and Geography**

The ancient land of **Egypt,** repeatedly referenced throughout the Hebrew Scriptures, occupies a region uniquely defined by one of the world's greatest natural features—the **Nile River**. Egypt's boundaries and geography played a decisive role in shaping its military strength, agricultural prosperity, and political interactions with neighboring nations, including Israel. Understanding the geographical features of Egypt is essential for appreciating its prominence in biblical history, especially in the narratives concerning **Abraham, Joseph, Moses,** and **Jeremiah**, where Egypt serves variously as a place of **refuge, enslavement, testing,** and **political intrigue**.

The land of Egypt in biblical times was commonly referred to by two main designations: **Mizraim** in Hebrew, reflecting the name of one of the sons of **Ham** (Genesis 10:6), and **Kemet** or **Kmt** in the native Egyptian tongue, meaning "the Black Land," a reference to the rich, dark soil of the Nile valley. The Greek term **Aigyptos**, from which the modern name "Egypt" derives, came into wider usage during the later classical period.

**Natural Boundaries of Egypt**

Egypt's geography was characterized by remarkably **stable and defensible borders** due to its surrounding natural barriers. These boundaries contributed to Egypt's historical longevity and relative insulation from foreign conquest for much of its early history.

- **North**: Egypt's northern boundary was the **Mediterranean Sea**, providing a natural maritime frontier and access to coastal trade with the Levant and beyond.
- **East**: To the east lay the **Sinai Peninsula**, a vast and difficult desert region punctuated by mountain ranges and wadis. This

eastern desert separated Egypt from the lands of **Canaan** and **Arabia**, functioning as both a protective barrier and the primary corridor through which military campaigns and migrations could occur. The biblical **Way of the Philistines** (Exodus 13:17) and other routes like the **Way of Shur** (Genesis 16:7; Exodus 15:22) crossed this zone.

- **South**: The southern boundary extended toward **Nubia** (ancient **Kush**), along the Nile, beyond the **First Cataract** at **Aswan**. This region was often contested, with Egypt periodically exerting control over **Nubian territories** and drawing gold, ivory, and other resources from these lands.
- **West**: Egypt's western limit merged into the **Libyan Desert**, a harsh and largely uninhabited expanse that discouraged significant military threat from that direction but served as home to nomadic tribes.

### The Nile: Egypt's Lifeline

Central to Egypt's geography is the **Nile River**, the longest river in the world, which flows northward from the heart of Africa to the Mediterranean Sea. The Nile's predictable **annual flooding** deposited nutrient-rich silt along its banks, making the narrow floodplain exceptionally fertile amidst otherwise arid surroundings. This natural irrigation sustained Egypt's agriculture and allowed for stable population growth, earning the land its reputation as the **"granary of the ancient world"** (cf. Genesis 41:47-49).

The Nile valley can be divided into two principal regions:

- **Upper Egypt**: The southern stretch of the Nile, running from the First Cataract northward toward **Memphis** (near modern Cairo). Characterized by a narrower river valley flanked by desert cliffs.
- **Lower Egypt**: The broad **Nile Delta** region in the north, where the river fans out into several distributaries before reaching the Mediterranean. This area included key cities such as **Tanis, Avaris, Pi-Ramesses**, and later **Zoan**.

The distinction between Upper and Lower Egypt was not only geographic but also political, with periods of history marked by the unification and division of these two regions under separate rulers.

The phrase **"from Migdol to Syene"** (Ezekiel 29:10; 30:6) is used in Scripture to describe Egypt's extent, referencing the border fortress of **Migdol** in the north and **Syene** (modern **Aswan**) at the southern frontier.

### Major Cities and Political Centers

Egypt's geopolitical influence was centered around several significant cities, each playing a role at different stages of biblical history:

- **Memphis**: Located near the junction of Upper and Lower Egypt, Memphis served as the political capital during much of the **Old Kingdom** and early Middle Kingdom periods.

- **Thebes**: Further south in Upper Egypt, Thebes (modern **Luxor**) rose to prominence during the **New Kingdom** (circa 1550–1070 B.C.E.), serving as a religious and administrative center.

- **Avaris and Pi-Ramesses**: Located in the eastern delta, Avaris was the capital during the **Hyksos period**, while **Pi-Ramesses**, possibly built upon Avaris' ruins, became a key city during the reign of **Ramesses II**. These cities are of particular interest in discussions of the **Israelite sojourn and enslavement**, as the Israelites are described as building **store cities for Pharaoh** (Exodus 1:11).

- **Zoan (Tanis)**: Mentioned in **Numbers 13:22** and **Psalm 78:12**, Zoan functioned as another administrative center in the delta and may have been connected to later periods of Egyptian-Israelite interaction.

### Egypt's Eastern Frontier and the Biblical Setting

The eastern delta region, including the **Wadi Tumilat**, was the likely area where the Israelites settled in the land of **Goshen** (Genesis 45:10; 47:4-6). Goshen's location near the Nile Delta provided both

**fertile pastureland for flocks** and proximity to **Egypt's eastern border defenses**, making it strategically significant.

This positioning also helps explain the **route of the Exodus**. The biblical narrative states that Jehovah did not lead the Israelites by the **Way of the Philistines**, though it was shorter, because of the military presence along that route (Exodus 13:17-18). Instead, the Israelites journeyed through the wilderness toward the **Red Sea (Yam Suph)**, with the **Sinai Peninsula** forming the key stage for their subsequent wanderings.

### Strategic Implications of Egypt's Geography

Egypt's boundaries and geographic features shaped its foreign policy and military activity. The defensibility of its borders allowed Egypt to maintain relative security at home while projecting military power into **Canaan, Syria, and Nubia** during various periods of expansion. Egyptian pharaohs often viewed Canaan as a **buffer zone** against northern threats, and their campaigns into the Levant frequently intersected with Israel's national life.

This geographical reality explains the continuous **tension between Egypt and Israel**, especially during the periods of the **Judges, the monarchy**, and the **prophets**. Egypt's involvement in the affairs of Judah, including its attempts to manipulate succession (2 Kings 23:29-35) and its role during the Babylonian crisis (Jeremiah 37–44), was made possible by these geographical proximities.

Egypt's agricultural surplus, made possible by the Nile, also made it an attractive refuge during times of famine, as seen when **Abraham** descended into Egypt (Genesis 12:10) and when **Jacob and his family** relocated during the famine of Joseph's time (Genesis 46:1-7).

The **boundaries and geography of Egypt** were central to its role in the biblical narrative. Shielded by deserts and sustained by the Nile, Egypt emerged as a dominant power with the capacity to influence the affairs of surrounding nations, including Israel. Its position as both a **source of refuge** and an **instrument of oppression** was conditioned by its natural defenses, agricultural wealth, and geopolitical location.

Understanding Egypt's geography allows for a clearer appreciation of how its power was felt throughout the biblical world, from the time of the patriarchs to the prophetic warnings of judgment. Jehovah's sovereign control over the land, seas, and nations ensured that Egypt, for all its might, would be used to accomplish His purposes, whether to shelter the patriarchs, discipline His people, or receive His judgments.

# CHAPTER 3 How Did the Nile Shape Egypt's Economy and Its Role in Biblical History?

**Economy Dependent on the Nile**

The economic life of ancient **Egypt** was inseparably tied to the presence and behavior of the **Nile River**, which flows northward from central Africa into the **Mediterranean Sea**. Without the Nile, Egypt would have been a barren desert, incapable of sustaining significant human settlement or economic productivity. With the Nile, however, Egypt became one of the most prosperous and enduring civilizations of the ancient world. This remarkable dependence on a single river system explains not only Egypt's material wealth but also its pivotal place in biblical events, including the **famine-driven migration of Abraham**, the **ascent of Joseph as a governor under Pharaoh**, the **enslavement of Israel**, and the **Egyptian involvement in Judah's political affairs during the monarchy**.

The **flooding of the Nile**, occurring annually between July and October, deposited rich silt along its banks, revitalizing the farmland and enabling Egypt to produce **abundant grain crops** year after year. This fertility gave rise to Egypt's reputation as a **"granary of the ancient world"**, a title well illustrated in the biblical record when Egypt served as the primary source of food during times of regional famine (Genesis 41:54-57). The Nile's predictable cycles of inundation and recession were not merely natural phenomena; they were integral to Egypt's economic stability, political power, and capacity to influence the surrounding nations.

The Israelites' interactions with Egypt occurred within this agricultural and economic context, and the Bible's portrayal of Egypt as both a **refuge in famine** and a **place of bondage** underscores how the prosperity of Egypt, rooted in the Nile, functioned as both a blessing and a snare.

**The Nile Flood Cycle and Agricultural Prosperity**

The **Nile flood cycle** was the central driver of Egyptian agriculture. Each year, heavy rains in the **Ethiopian Highlands** swelled the **Blue Nile**, which, together with the **White Nile**, brought an annual inundation to the Egyptian river valley. As the floodwaters receded, they left behind a layer of **nutrient-rich alluvial soil**, ideal for growing a variety of crops, particularly **emmer wheat** and **barley**, which formed the staples of the Egyptian diet.

The biblical account in **Genesis 41** records that Pharaoh's dreams of **seven fat cows and seven thin cows**, along with **seven healthy ears of grain and seven thin ears**, were interpreted by **Joseph** as predictive of **seven years of plenty followed by seven years of famine**. This interpretation directly reflects the centrality of agriculture in Egypt's economy and the importance of the Nile's cycles. Joseph's plan to **store grain during the years of abundance** capitalized on the Nile's productivity and allowed Egypt not only to survive the famine but to profit from it, extending its influence over neighboring peoples who were forced to buy grain from Egyptian granaries.

This event is not merely historical but theologically significant. It demonstrates Jehovah's sovereignty, working through natural processes and human agency (Joseph) to provide deliverance for **Jacob's household**, preserving the line through which the promised **seed** (Genesis 3:15) would come.

### Irrigation and Land Management

The agricultural success of Egypt was not solely dependent on the natural flooding of the Nile. Over centuries, the Egyptians developed sophisticated **irrigation systems**, including:

- **Canals** to direct water into fields beyond the immediate floodplain.
- **Basins** that could hold floodwater for gradual release.
- **Shadufs**, simple water-lifting devices used to irrigate higher ground.

This water management allowed for **multiple harvests annually** in some regions, further enhancing Egypt's economic power. The system of **measuring the inundation levels** at **Nileometers** located at various points along the river ensured that the government could assess crop potential and set appropriate taxation rates. Egyptian taxation was often paid in the form of agricultural produce, reinforcing the government's control over economic life.

This centralized control is reflected in the biblical narrative where, after interpreting Pharaoh's dreams, **Joseph's administration of grain storage and distribution** effectively centralized the food supply under royal authority (Genesis 41:47-49; 47:13-26). Joseph's measures included the collection of surplus grain into **storehouses** located in various cities, ensuring survival during the famine and leading to the consolidation of **land ownership under Pharaoh** as farmers sold their lands to obtain food.

### Livestock and Secondary Agricultural Industries

In addition to cereal agriculture, Egypt's economy benefited from **livestock raising**, particularly cattle, sheep, and goats. The Nile's delta region, with its grassy marshlands, provided excellent pastureland. However, **Genesis 46:34** records that shepherds were regarded as **abhorrent to the Egyptians**, suggesting both cultural and economic tensions between Egypt's agriculturally focused population and the pastoralist lifestyle of the Israelites.

Livestock were not only sources of meat and milk but also of **hides, wool, and labor** for plowing and transportation. The biblical description of Israel's flocks and herds during their sojourn in Goshen (Genesis 47:1-6) highlights that they were settled in an area favorable to such pastoral activities, without threatening Egypt's dominant agricultural economy.

Other economic activities linked to the Nile included **papyrus harvesting** for writing materials, **flax cultivation** for linen production, and **fishing**, particularly in the Nile's delta and marshlands. These industries contributed to Egypt's economic diversification, allowing it to trade widely with neighboring regions.

### Trade Networks and Economic Expansion

Egypt's agricultural surplus, enabled by the Nile, facilitated its extensive **trade networks**. Goods produced in Egypt were exchanged for luxury items and resources unavailable locally, such as:

- **Cedar wood** from Lebanon.
- **Copper and turquoise** from the Sinai Peninsula.
- **Gold and ivory** from Nubia.
- **Frankincense and myrrh** from Punt (possibly modern Somalia or Eritrea).
- **Horses and chariots**, later mentioned in connection with Solomon's dealings (1 Kings 10:28-29).

These trade connections not only enriched Egypt but also brought it into continual contact—and conflict—with other powers in the Levant, including the **Canaanite city-states** and eventually **Israel and Judah**.

This economic dominance is a key backdrop to understanding Egypt's attractiveness as a **refuge during times of crisis** (as for Abraham and Jacob) and its persistent role as a **tempting but unreliable political ally** during the prophetic period, particularly in the time of **Jeremiah**, when Judah looked to Egypt for help against Babylon (Jeremiah 37:5-10).

### Egypt's Economic Resilience and Vulnerabilities

While the Nile provided a stable foundation for Egypt's economy, the biblical narrative and historical records both indicate that Egypt was not immune to **economic vulnerabilities**, particularly in times of **low inundation** or **regional drought**. The seven years of famine during Joseph's administration reflect just such a period of crisis, which magnified Egypt's dependence on proper management of its natural resources.

Additionally, the agricultural economy's reliance on the Nile meant that any significant disruption to the river's flow—whether by climate change, military conquest, or administrative failure—could lead to social and political instability. Egyptian history records several periods of **internal collapse** during the **First and Second**

# THE EGYPTIAN EMPIRE

**Intermediate Periods**, often associated with **failure of the Nile floods** and consequent famine.

This backdrop adds further weight to the biblical accounts, situating the patriarchal narratives and the Exodus events within a historical context of both **prosperity and vulnerability**, underlining that Egypt's apparent strength could be—and was—overthrown by Jehovah's direct intervention.

The **economy of Egypt**, wholly dependent on the **Nile River**, was the foundation of its wealth, political stability, and military strength throughout antiquity. The annual flood cycle, agricultural abundance, and intricate irrigation systems created an environment where Egypt could serve as both **a place of refuge for the patriarchs** and **an oppressor of Israel during their enslavement**.

The biblical narratives are firmly rooted in this historical reality, reflecting an accurate understanding of Egypt's economy long before modern archaeological discovery confirmed such details. The **prosperity of Egypt**, while often presenting itself as a source of security, was ultimately shown in Scripture to be **subject to Jehovah's sovereign control**, who alone could sustain or overthrow nations according to His righteous will.

# CHAPTER 4 What Were the Principal Products of Egypt, and How Did They Shape Its Role in Biblical History?

### Products

The **economy of ancient Egypt**, grounded in the fertility of the **Nile River**, yielded a wealth of agricultural and manufactured products that not only sustained the local population but also enabled Egypt to become one of the primary trading powers of the ancient world. Egypt's natural abundance, coupled with its geographical placement at the crossroads of major trade routes, made it a central supplier of goods to the Mediterranean basin, the Levant, and beyond. The products of Egypt frequently appear in the biblical record, shaping the experiences of the patriarchs, the Israelites in captivity, and later international relations throughout the monarchy and prophetic periods.

The productivity of Egypt was a key factor in its political stability and economic strength, but more importantly, it explains why Egypt so often became a **place of refuge during times of famine**, as in the cases of **Abraham** and **Jacob**, and why Egypt's power tempted Israel and Judah into **unwise political alliances**, leading to prophetic rebuke. This section explores the major products of Egypt as attested both by Scripture and by archaeological findings, demonstrating the historical accuracy of the biblical descriptions.

### Grains and Agricultural Staples

At the heart of Egypt's economy was its **agricultural output**, particularly the cultivation of grains made possible by the **Nile's annual inundation**. Egypt's principal grain crops were:

- **Barley**: Frequently mentioned in Scripture and used for making bread and beer, staples of the Egyptian diet.

- **Wheat**: Especially **emmer wheat** and **spelt** (a type of wheat), crucial for breadmaking and a primary foodstuff for the population (Exodus 9:31-32).
- **Flax**: Cultivated for its fibers, which were processed into **linen**, one of Egypt's most prized export products. Egyptian linen was renowned for its fineness and appears in Scripture as an item of luxury (Proverbs 7:16; Ezekiel 27:7).

The **importance of grain production** is repeatedly emphasized in the biblical narrative. During the **seven years of famine** interpreted by **Joseph** from Pharaoh's dreams, Egypt's storehouses of grain became the salvation of surrounding lands, including **Canaan** (Genesis 41:47-57). Egypt's capacity to stockpile surplus grain underscores the nation's agricultural resilience, positioning it as a regional supplier in times of crisis.

This agricultural wealth explains why **grain ships from Egypt**, such as the one mentioned in **Acts 27:5-6, 38** that carried **Paul** as a prisoner, regularly transported grain to **Italy** and other Mediterranean destinations, confirming Egypt's long-standing reputation as the **granary of the ancient world**.

### Fruits, Vegetables, and Luxuries of the Land

Beyond grains, Egypt produced a rich variety of **fruits, vegetables, and herbs**, many of which are referenced directly in Scripture:

- **Vineyards** produced grapes for wine (Genesis 40:9-11).
- **Date palms**, **fig trees**, and **pomegranates** were cultivated throughout Egypt's fertile regions.
- **Vegetable gardens** yielded cucumbers, watermelons, leeks, onions, and garlic, items nostalgically recalled by the Israelites during their wilderness wanderings (Numbers 11:5; 20:5).

These foods contributed not only to the sustenance of Egypt's population but also to the image of Egypt as a place of plenty and comfort, contrasting sharply with the barrenness of the wilderness. The Israelites' complaint in **Numbers 11:5** reflects the psychological power of Egypt's agricultural richness, demonstrating how material abundance can become spiritually dangerous when it fosters discontent and forgetfulness of divine provision.

**Papyrus: Egypt's Writing Material Export**

Another significant product of Egypt was **papyrus**, the reedy plant that thrived in the **marshes of the Nile Delta** (Exodus 2:3; Job 8:11). Papyrus stems were harvested, cut into strips, pressed, and dried to form sheets used for writing material. This innovation made Egypt the ancient world's primary producer of writing surfaces, contributing greatly to the spread of administrative, literary, and religious texts across the Mediterranean and Near Eastern regions.

Papyrus not only supplied domestic needs but was also a valuable export item, playing a role in Egypt's international trade network. The prevalence of papyrus in ancient Egyptian documentation—whether contracts, letters, or religious inscriptions—underscores its importance in maintaining the **bureaucratic efficiency** for which Egypt became known.

**Livestock and Animal Products**

**Stock raising** was another important sector of Egypt's economy. The biblical record notes that **Abraham** acquired **sheep, cattle, asses, camels, and servants** while sojourning in Egypt (Genesis 12:16), demonstrating the wealth and prominence of Egyptian livestock industries.

- **Cattle** were especially valued, symbolizing wealth and used in plowing, transport, and sacrifice.
- **Sheep and goats** provided wool, milk, meat, and hides.
- **Asses and camels** were employed as beasts of burden, facilitating trade and transportation across desert routes.
- **Horses**, first mentioned during **Joseph's administration** (Genesis 47:17), became particularly significant in Egyptian military and commercial life, introduced likely from **Asia** and later renowned throughout the region for their quality. Egyptian horses and **chariots** became major export items by the time of **Solomon** (1 Kings 10:28-29).

The Egyptians also managed **poultry** and **waterfowl**, including geese, ducks, and pigeons, depicted frequently in tomb paintings. The Nile's ecosystem supported abundant **fish stocks** (Isaiah 19:8), and fishing was a widespread occupation.

Egypt's fauna also included **hippopotamuses** and **crocodiles**, the latter of which is symbolically associated with Egypt's pride in **Ezekiel 29:3-5**, where Pharaoh is likened to a great river monster. **Birds of prey**, scavengers, and other wildlife, including jackals, hyenas, lions, snakes, and lizards, populated the desert margins and wilderness zones.

### Minerals and Metalwork

Though Egypt lacked significant forests, requiring the **import of cedar and timber from Phoenicia** (Tyre and Sidon), it possessed substantial mineral resources. The hills along the **Red Sea** and **Sinai Peninsula** contained:

- **Gold mines**, providing wealth that contributed to Egypt's luxury industries (Genesis 13:2).
- **Copper mines**, essential for the production of **bronze** tools and weapons.
- **Turquoise and malachite** deposits, used for jewelry and decoration.

Egyptian metallurgy, particularly in bronze production, played a role in the region's arms trade and craftsmanship. Egyptian artisans produced fine **bronze tools, ornaments, and weaponry**, which were exported alongside other goods.

The use of **granite, limestone, and alabaster** from Egyptian quarries also facilitated monumental construction, including temples, tombs, and obelisks. The use of **mud brick** for ordinary housing and even royal palaces, as reflected in the biblical reference to **Israelite forced labor in brickmaking** (Exodus 1:14), shows the integration of local materials into Egypt's building economy.

### Trade Goods and International Influence

The surplus generated by Egypt's agricultural and craft industries allowed for extensive **international trade**, making Egypt a major participant in the commercial networks of the ancient world. Egypt exported:

- **Grain**, especially during times of famine in neighboring regions.
- **Linen garments**, prized for their quality and often dyed in various colors (Ezekiel 27:7).
- **Papyrus sheets** as writing materials.
- **Chariots and horses**, significant military goods in demand throughout the Near East.
- **Bronze goods** and jewelry crafted from native and imported metals.

In return, Egypt imported:

- **Cedar wood** from Phoenicia.
- **Silver**, **copper**, and **tin** from Anatolia and Cyprus.
- **Precious stones** from the Sinai and Nubia.
- **Frankincense and myrrh** from southern Arabia or eastern Africa.
- **Slaves**, both from military conquest and from the broader slave trade.

These exchanges illustrate why Egypt was both a desirable ally and a dangerous entanglement for Israel, especially in periods when Judah's kings looked to Egypt for military or political support rather than trusting in Jehovah (Isaiah 30:1-5; Jeremiah 2:18-19).

The product wealth of Egypt—centered on its **agricultural abundance, livestock resources, metal industries**, and **international trade connections**—formed the backbone of its economic strength throughout the biblical period. Egypt's status as the **granary of the ancient world** and supplier of luxury goods positioned it as a place of both **material blessing and spiritual temptation** for Israel.

# THE EGYPTIAN EMPIRE

The biblical record accurately reflects these economic realities, demonstrating once again the **historical reliability of Scripture** and the consistent message that **material prosperity cannot substitute for covenant faithfulness**. Egypt's products contributed to its allure, but its trust in **earthly abundance and false gods** ultimately brought it into conflict with the purposes of Jehovah, who alone provides true security and sustenance.

# CHAPTER 5 Who Were the People of Egypt in Biblical Times?

**The People**

The identity and composition of the **Egyptian people** throughout the biblical period are integral to understanding Egypt's role in the history of Israel. Scripture presents Egypt not only as a geopolitical entity but as a nation whose **ethnic origins**, **social structures**, and **internal divisions** directly influenced its relationship with Jehovah's covenant people. Far from being a homogeneous group, the Egyptians were a **composite population**, reflecting the complex history of migrations, tribal developments, and political unifications that shaped Egypt from the earliest postdiluvian generations onward.

The Bible identifies the Egyptians as **descendants of Ham**, specifically through **Mizraim**, one of the sons of Ham (Genesis 10:6). This genealogical origin places Egypt within the broader family of Hamitic peoples, alongside **Cush**, **Put**, and **Canaan**. While Egypt's geographical proximity to Semitic peoples in the Levant and its long history of interaction with Nubians from the south introduced considerable ethnic diversity, the fundamental biblical testimony maintains Egypt's Hamitic descent as a core aspect of its identity.

Understanding the people of Egypt, their ethnic origins, social organization, and cultural distinctions, provides essential background for the biblical narratives of **Abraham's sojourn**, **Joseph's rise to power**, **Israel's enslavement and exodus**, and **Jeremiah's prophetic confrontations** with Egyptian kings.

**Hamitic Descent Through Mizraim**

The **Table of Nations** in **Genesis 10** offers the primary biblical framework for identifying the Egyptian people:

"The sons of Ham: Cush, Mizraim, Put, and Canaan." (Genesis 10:6)

# THE EGYPTIAN EMPIRE

Mizraim, the Hebrew term commonly translated as **Egypt**, serves both as the name of the ancestor and the land itself. The dual form of the word in Hebrew (*Mizraim*) may reflect the historical division between **Upper and Lower Egypt**, suggesting an early awareness of Egypt's internal geographic and political bifurcation. The descendants of Mizraim are further listed as:

"The Ludim, Anamim, Lehabim, Naphtuhim, Pathrusim, Casluhim (from whom the Philistines came), and Caphtorim." (Genesis 10:13-14)

Several of these subgroups, such as the **Pathrusim**, are associated with specific regions within Egypt. **Pathros**, from which Pathrusim derives, is explicitly identified with **Upper Egypt** (Isaiah 11:11; Jeremiah 44:1, 15; Ezekiel 29:14). Some evidence suggests the **Naphtuhim** were located in the **Nile Delta region**, although exact identifications remain challenging due to the lack of clear archaeological correlation for all these tribal names.

The biblical identification of the Egyptians as **Hamitic** stands in contrast to many modern reference works that often describe the Egyptians as **Semitic-speaking** due to their later adoption of Semitic linguistic elements. However, as discussed previously, **ethnic descent and language adoption are not synonymous**, and the biblical account remains reliable in affirming the Egyptians' Hamitic origins.

### Composite Ethnic Structure and Tribal Origins

The political and social landscape of ancient Egypt further supports the biblical view of a **composite population formed from various family tribes**. Historically, Egypt was divided into numerous regional units known as **nomes**—administrative districts that existed from the earliest periods of Egyptian civilization and persisted until its final dynastic phases. There were typically **42 nomes: 20 in Lower Egypt** (the northern delta region) and **22 in Upper Egypt** (the southern Nile valley).

These divisions were not purely geographic but also reflected the **tribal composition and local identities** of Egypt's peoples. Even after Egypt was unified under a central monarchy—traditionally attributed to **Narmer (Menes)** at the beginning of the **First Dynasty** (circa 3100 B.C.E.)—the nomes retained their distinct identities, religious centers, and local governance. When the **central government weakened**, as occurred during the **First Intermediate Period** (circa 2181–2055 B.C.E.) and the **Second Intermediate Period** (circa 1782–1570 B.C.E.), Egypt often fractured along these ancient lines, splitting into **Upper and Lower Egypt** or even fragmenting into numerous **petty kingdoms** aligned with individual nomes.

The persistence of these divisions suggests an enduring recognition of **tribal and familial roots** among the Egyptian people, supporting the biblical description of Egypt's descent from multiple Hamitic family lines.

### Physical Appearance and Racial Diversity

Ancient Egyptian art, mummified remains, and written records provide additional evidence regarding the physical characteristics of the Egyptian people. Wall paintings, statuary, and funerary artifacts depict Egyptians as generally **slender and small-statured**, with complexions ranging from **light brown to dark brown**, and with **straight or curly hair**. These artistic conventions are consistent across many centuries, though with considerable variety, reflecting both the **northern Delta populations** and the **southern Upper Egyptian and Nubian interactions**.

Archaeological and anthropological studies confirm this **range of phenotypic diversity**. Egypt's position as a **crossroads between Africa and Asia** ensured a continual flow of people through migration, conquest, and trade, contributing to the variation seen in depictions of Egyptians and their neighbors. However, the consistent portrayal of Egyptians as distinct from **Nubians to the south** and **Asiatics to the northeast** underscores the Egyptians' own sense of unique identity, in line with their Hamitic lineage through Mizraim.

Despite the influences from surrounding peoples, including the presence of **Semitic workers, slaves, and merchants** within Egypt—such as the **Israelites during their sojourn and enslavement**—Egypt retained its core identity as a people descended from Mizraim, with the biblical witness remaining the most reliable genealogical record of their origins.

### Social Structure and Class Distinctions

The **social organization** of ancient Egypt reflected a highly stratified society, with sharp distinctions between classes. The population consisted of:

- **The Pharaoh and Royal Household**: Seen as divine or semi-divine, Pharaoh was not only king but also the religious high priest, regarded as the living representative of the gods, particularly **Ra** or **Amun** in later periods.
- **The Nobility and Priesthood**: These elites managed both the administration of the state and the religious institutions. Priests held significant power, especially during the periods when temples amassed considerable wealth.
- **Scribes and Officials**: As literacy was not widespread, scribes formed an essential professional class, managing the bureaucracy and recordkeeping that sustained Egypt's complex economy and governance.
- **Artisans and Craftsmen**: These skilled laborers produced goods for both domestic use and export, including linen textiles, pottery, metalwork, and stone carving.
- **Farmers and Laborers**: The majority of the Egyptian population were agricultural workers, dependent on the Nile's cycles for their livelihood.
- **Slaves and Foreign Captives**: Among the lowest social classes were slaves, including prisoners of war, debt slaves, and foreign captives. The **Israelite population during the time of the Exodus** fell into this category, subjected to **forced labor in brickmaking and construction** (Exodus 1:13-14).

The biblical account accurately reflects these class distinctions, particularly the role of **Joseph as an official** in Pharaoh's administration and the status of the **Israelites as oppressed laborers** under later Pharaohs.

### Religious Identity and National Distinctiveness

Ethnically and culturally, the Egyptians were also defined by their **religious worldview**, which pervaded every level of their society. The worship of a vast pantheon of gods—including **Ra, Osiris, Isis, Horus**, and **Amun**—sustained not only religious life but also political legitimacy for Pharaoh. The **idolatry of Egypt** is repeatedly condemned in Scripture (Exodus 12:12; Ezekiel 30:13), and its gods were shown to be powerless in the face of Jehovah's might during the **ten plagues** (Exodus 7–12).

The theological contrast between Egypt's **polytheism** and Israel's **exclusive devotion to Jehovah** shaped the spiritual struggle that accompanied the historical interactions between the two nations. Egypt's religious identity was inseparable from its sense of ethnic distinction, reinforcing its role as both **oppressor of Israel** and **object of divine judgment**.

The people of Egypt, descended from **Mizraim**, formed a **complex and composite population** whose tribal origins, social divisions, and religious distinctiveness shaped their historical role in the biblical narrative. The ethnic diversity visible in Egypt's art and anthropology does not contradict the biblical account of Hamitic descent but rather illustrates the predictable outcome of a people long positioned at the intersection of major trade routes and migration paths.

Throughout their history, the Egyptians maintained their unique identity amid external influences, standing as a significant and enduring power that repeatedly intersected with the history of Jehovah's people. Their internal divisions, reflected in the ancient nomes and the persistent separation between Upper and Lower Egypt, echo the genealogical fragmentation implied in the post-Babel dispersal.

The biblical record, far from offering an idealized or simplistic view of Egypt, presents a **historically grounded and theologically meaningful portrait** of a nation whose people, for all their strength and sophistication, remained subject to the sovereignty of Jehovah, the one true God of heaven and earth.

# CHAPTER 6 What Do We Know About the Language of the Egyptians in Biblical Times?

### Language

The **language of ancient Egypt**, like its people, stands distinct among the tongues of the ancient Near East. The biblical testimony identifies the Egyptians as **descendants of Ham through Mizraim** (Genesis 10:6), and this genealogical reality is consistent with the linguistic evidence that places Egyptian outside the family of **Semitic languages**, though with certain similarities in structure and vocabulary. While modern linguistic scholars have at times classified Egyptian under broader groupings such as **"Hamito-Semitic"** or **"Afro-Asiatic,"** the prevailing scholarly conclusion acknowledges that **Egyptian stands apart as an independent branch**, not properly counted among the Semitic languages despite some shared features.

The biblical narrative itself affirms the distinctiveness of the Egyptian tongue. In **Genesis 42:23**, during the encounter between **Joseph** and his brothers, we are told that:

"They did not know that Joseph understood them, for there was an interpreter between them."

This straightforward detail confirms that during the time of **Joseph's administration (circa 1737–1657 B.C.E.)**, Egyptian was sufficiently different from the Hebrew spoken by the sons of **Jacob** that communication required an intermediary. This fact alone offers strong support for the view that Egyptian was not a Semitic language in the conventional sense but a separate tongue, reflecting the Hamitic ancestry of the Egyptians.

### Egyptian and Its Linguistic Classification

The classification of ancient Egyptian remains a subject of linguistic analysis, but even leading Egyptologists, such as **Sir Alan**

**Gardiner**, have maintained that Egyptian is not Semitic. In his **Egyptian Grammar (1957, p. 3)**, Gardiner states:

"Egyptian differs from all the Semitic tongues a good deal more than any one of them differs from any other, and at least until its relationship to the African languages is more closely defined, Egyptian must certainly be classified as standing outside the Semitic group."

This conclusion harmonizes well with the biblical account of **the confusion of languages at Babel** (Genesis 11:1-9), where Jehovah divided human speech into distinct linguistic families. Egypt, as one of the principal postdiluvian civilizations, developed a tongue separate from its Semitic neighbors, though centuries of interaction led to **some borrowing of vocabulary and structural features**.

The modern linguistic term **"Afro-Asiatic"** often encompasses both Hamitic and Semitic languages, but such classifications are constructed primarily on shared features rather than strict genealogical lines. The Bible's genealogical framework remains the most reliable source for determining the true ethnic and linguistic affiliations of the Egyptian people.

**Writing Systems: Hieroglyphic, Hieratic, and Demotic**

Central to understanding the Egyptian language is its system of **writing**, which provides most of the surviving evidence for the structure of the tongue, though with significant challenges in fully reconstructing its phonology.

The Egyptians employed **hieroglyphic writing**, a complex system of pictographic symbols representing objects, animals, people, and abstract concepts. These symbols could function as:

- **Logograms**: Symbols representing entire words or ideas.
- **Phonograms**: Symbols representing sounds, often consonants or syllables.
- **Determinatives**: Silent signs used to clarify the meaning of words.

Despite the inclusion of phonograms, Egyptian writing was never entirely phonetic. The **precise pronunciation** of ancient Egyptian words remains largely speculative, as the hieroglyphic system provides limited vowel information. What is known today comes mainly from **later transcriptions in Greek**, **Aramaic**, and especially **Coptic**, the last phase of the Egyptian language spoken from the **third century C.E. onward**.

While **hieroglyphic inscriptions** were typically reserved for monumental and religious texts, Egyptian scribes developed more practical cursive scripts for everyday use:

1. **Hieratic**: A simplified, cursive form of hieroglyphics used primarily by priests and scribes for administrative documents, written with ink on **papyrus** or **leather**.

2. **Demotic**: Emerging around the **seventh century B.C.E.**, demotic was an even more abbreviated script used for commercial, legal, and literary texts.

The ability to decipher these scripts was lost for centuries until the discovery of the **Rosetta Stone** in **1799**, which contained a decree in **three scripts**: hieroglyphic, demotic, and Greek. The Greek inscription provided the key to unlocking the meaning of the hieroglyphic and demotic texts, a breakthrough achieved through the work of **Jean-François Champollion** in the early 19th century.

### Challenges in Reconstructing Ancient Egyptian Phonology

One of the significant obstacles in fully understanding the Egyptian language, especially during the earlier periods relevant to the biblical narratives, is the **lack of clear vocalization** in the hieroglyphic system. Vowels were typically not written, and consonantal usage alone does not provide sufficient evidence to reconstruct exact pronunciations.

Reconstruction efforts rely heavily on:

- **Coptic pronunciation**, which, though separated by centuries, retains traces of earlier Egyptian sounds.
- **Greek and Aramaic transcriptions of Egyptian names and terms**, providing external clues to phonetic values.

- **Comparative analysis** with known Semitic and African languages, though this remains speculative given the isolation of Egyptian within the linguistic landscape.

Because no inscriptions of other ancient Hamitic languages survive from the second millennium B.C.E. or earlier, comparative data is limited. This reality underscores the **unique status of Egyptian as the only well-documented early Hamitic tongue** and supports the biblical account of separate language families emerging from Babel.

### Loanwords and Linguistic Interaction

Although Egyptian remained distinct, **linguistic borrowing** occurred through prolonged contact with Semitic peoples. Some **Egyptian loanwords** entered Hebrew and other Semitic languages, particularly terms relating to **government administration, architecture, and agriculture**. Examples may include words for **measuring units, titles of officials**, and **types of grain or textiles**.

Similarly, Egyptian adopted certain Semitic elements, especially during periods of **Hyksos domination** (circa 1650–1550 B.C.E.) when Semitic-speaking rulers held power in the Nile Delta. However, such borrowing does not equate to full linguistic assimilation.

The example of **Joseph using an interpreter** (Genesis 42:23) confirms that even in official contexts, Egyptian maintained its distinctiveness as a language separate from the speech of the Semitic patriarchs.

### Theological Implications: Babel and Linguistic Diversity

The evidence from Egyptian language and writing provides a striking affirmation of the **biblical account of the division of languages at Babel**. Egypt's distinct tongue, unlike the surrounding Semitic dialects, stands as a testimony to Jehovah's intervention in human history to prevent the consolidation of rebellious humanity under one speech (Genesis 11:1-9).

This divine action produced real and lasting separation among peoples, reflected not only in genealogical descent but also in **linguistic divergence**. Egypt's maintenance of a separate language for millennia, even amid regional interaction, underscores the integrity of the Genesis narrative and highlights the sovereignty of Jehovah in directing the course of nations.

The **language of ancient Egypt**, though exhibiting occasional affinities with Semitic tongues, was fundamentally **Hamitic** in origin, distinct and separate from the languages of Israel and its Semitic neighbors. The biblical detail of **Joseph's need for an interpreter** corroborates this distinction and aligns with the broader theological framework of **linguistic division after Babel**.

Egypt's elaborate writing systems—**hieroglyphic, hieratic, and demotic**—attest to the complexity and sophistication of its civilization, while the difficulty in fully reconstructing ancient Egyptian pronunciation highlights the limitations of human knowledge and the enduring accuracy of Scripture in testifying to the uniqueness of the Egyptian people and their speech.

The study of Egypt's language, far from undermining the biblical witness, provides further confirmation that **the history of Israel unfolded within a real and accurately described cultural and linguistic environment**, governed at every point by the hand of Jehovah.

Edward D. Andrews

# What Was the Nature of Egyptian Religion in Biblical Times?

**Religion**

The religious environment of **ancient Egypt** was characterized by **extreme polytheism**, superstition, and the pervasive influence of occult practices. Far from being a spiritually enlightened culture, Egypt embodied the religious confusion that arose after the **dispersion at Babel** (Genesis 11:1-9), manifesting in a labyrinth of **gods, goddesses, magical rituals, and priestly hierarchies**. Egypt's religious system stood in direct contrast to the **monotheistic worship of Jehovah**, whose purity and exclusivity are consistently affirmed throughout Scripture. Egypt's idolatry, therefore, was not merely a foreign religion—it represented a direct challenge to the true God, a defiance that brought upon the nation repeated rebukes and judgments from Jehovah through His prophets and servants.

The prevalence of polytheism in Egypt, alongside magic, spiritism, and ceremonial idolatry, underscores the **spiritual darkness** into which the patriarchs descended when they entered Egypt, whether in Abraham's sojourn (Genesis 12:10), Joseph's elevation under Pharaoh (Genesis 41:41-46), the Israelites' bondage (Exodus 1), or Jeremiah's later confrontations with Pharaoh's house (Jeremiah 46). Egypt's religious worldview was not a neutral backdrop; it was a potent force shaping the nation's culture, politics, and interactions with Israel.

**Polytheism and the Proliferation of Deities**

Egyptian religion, from its earliest records through the biblical periods, was marked by the **worship of hundreds of gods and goddesses**. Every city and town possessed its **local patron deity**, often bearing the title **"Lord of the City"**. A funerary list from the tomb of **Thutmose III** records **approximately 740 gods**, illustrating the overwhelming multiplicity of Egypt's pantheon. The fragmentation of religious belief, coupled with the regional diversity of deities, reflected not only the composite nature of Egypt's population but also the chaotic religious legacy of post-Babel human society.

# THE EGYPTIAN EMPIRE

The biblical judgment against **"all the gods of Egypt"** (Exodus 12:12) during the tenth plague demonstrates Jehovah's complete rejection of this polytheistic system. Far from being isolated to specific cult centers, Egypt's gods were woven into daily life, agricultural practices, political authority, and national identity.

Among the most prominent Egyptian deities were:

- **Ra (Re)**: The **sun god**, often considered the source of life and the ruler of the heavens.

- **Amon (Amun)**: Elevated later as **"king of the gods"** under the compound name **Amon-Ra**, especially at Thebes (biblical **No**, Jeremiah 46:25).

- **Osiris**: God of the underworld and afterlife, husband of **Isis**, and father of **Horus**. Osiris represented death, resurrection, and fertility.

- **Isis**: Mother goddess associated with fertility, magic, and motherhood.

- **Horus**: Often depicted as a falcon-headed god, symbolizing kingship and the sky.

- **Ptah, Thoth, Anubis, Hathor, Sobek**, and many others, representing various aspects of nature, human activities, and cosmic order.

These gods were frequently grouped into **triads or trinities**, consisting of a **father god, mother goddess**, and **son**. Yet, unlike the unity of Jehovah, these so-called "triads" were often **hierarchically inconsistent**—in many cases, the son or the goddess wielded greater influence than the father. The goddess often remained the **principal deity**, with the father taking a subordinate role as "prince consort." This inversion of divine hierarchy stood in stark contrast to the biblical portrayal of **Jehovah as the supreme Father and sovereign Creator** (Isaiah 45:5-7).

### The Divine Kingship of Pharaoh

Egypt's political structure was inseparably linked to its religious beliefs through the **deification of Pharaoh**. The Egyptian king was regarded not merely as a ruler but as the **living embodiment of the divine**, often styled as the **son of Ra** and the mediator between the gods and the people. This belief endowed Pharaoh with **absolute religious and political authority**, positioning him as a central figure in the maintenance of cosmic order (*ma'at*).

This divine kingship forms the background for Pharaoh's arrogant response to **Moses and Aaron**:

"Who is Jehovah, so that I should obey his voice to let Israel go? I do not know Jehovah, and moreover, I will not let Israel go." (Exodus 5:2)

Pharaoh's rejection of Jehovah was not mere political stubbornness; it reflected the core of Egyptian religious ideology that **Pharaoh himself was a god**. The confrontation between Moses and Pharaoh was therefore not simply a contest between two leaders but a direct **challenge between the false gods of Egypt and the true God of Israel**.

### Ritual Practices and Priestly Hierarchies

The service of Egypt's gods was conducted by an extensive **priestly class**, who maintained the daily rituals necessary to appease and sustain their deities. Unlike Israelite worship, where Jehovah desired the heartfelt devotion of the entire nation (Deuteronomy 6:4-5), Egyptian religion restricted access to the inner sanctums of temples to the **priests alone**. These priests performed elaborate ceremonies, including:

- **Awakening the god** each morning with hymns.
- **Washing, dressing, and "feeding"** the idol image.
- Conducting processions and festivals, where the god's image would be **paraded through the streets** and the people would receive merit merely by witnessing the spectacle.

The practice of **feeding the gods** with offerings of food, drink, and incense highlights the contrast with Jehovah, who declares:

"If I were hungry, I would not tell you, for the world and all it contains are mine." (Psalm 50:12)

This ritual dependence of the Egyptian gods upon human service underscores their **false and powerless nature**, in contrast to the self-sufficient and eternal Creator revealed in Scripture (Isaiah 40:28).

### Magic, Spiritism, and Superstition

Integral to Egyptian religion was its **embrace of magic, spells, amulets, and spiritistic practices**. Magic was not considered separate from religion; it was part of the priestly and everyday religious system. Ancient texts such as the **Book of the Dead** contain incantations and spells designed to aid the deceased in the afterlife, and magic was employed to:

- Ward off disease.
- Secure blessings.
- Bind or manipulate spiritual forces.

The Bible acknowledges this magical culture in **Genesis 41:8**, where **Pharaoh's magicians and wise men** are called upon to interpret his dreams, a task they failed to accomplish until **Joseph**, empowered by Jehovah, provided the true meaning.

Egypt's **magicians and sorcerers** also feature in the confrontation with Moses and Aaron, initially **duplicating some of the signs and wonders** (Exodus 7:11-22), though they eventually confessed:

"This is the finger of God." (Exodus 8:19)

Their inability to replicate Jehovah's power demonstrated the **limitations and deception of their magical arts**.

The widespread use of **amulets, lucky charms, and magical inscriptions** on papyrus further reveals the superstitious heart of Egyptian religion. Spirit mediums, necromancers, and professional foretellers of events were prominent, directly violating the standards Jehovah set for His people (Deuteronomy 18:10-12).

### Regional Variation and Contradictions Among the Gods

One of the striking features of Egyptian religion was its **lack of doctrinal unity**. Various regions maintained their own **primary**

**deities**, and often the myths, genealogies, and functions of these gods **contradicted one another**. For example:

- The sun god could be **Ra, Aton,** or **Horus**, depending on the locality.
- The creator god might be **Ptah** in **Memphis, Amon** in **Thebes,** or **Khnum** at **Elephantine**.
- The god **Ra** was known under **at least 75 different names and forms**, adding to the confusion.

This fragmentation reflects the inherent instability of polytheistic systems, as opposed to the **unity and consistency of Jehovah's revelation** through His inspired Word.

The prominent triad of **Osiris, Isis, and Horus** was widespread but not uniformly accepted across Egypt. Similarly, the elevation of **Amon-Ra** as "king of the gods" was a political-religious development tied to Thebes' dominance, rather than universal theological conviction.

### Theological Contrast and Divine Judgment

The contest between Jehovah and the gods of Egypt reached its climax in the **Exodus narrative**, where each of the **ten plagues** systematically undermined the authority of specific Egyptian deities:

- **The Nile turned to blood** challenged **Hapi**, the Nile god.
- **Darkness over the land** defied **Ra**, the sun god.
- **The death of the firstborn** delivered the ultimate blow, targeting the **divine status of Pharaoh himself** and exposing the impotence of Egypt's pantheon.

Jehovah's statement concerning the plagues was explicit:

"On all the gods of Egypt I will execute judgments. I am Jehovah." (Exodus 12:12)

This divine judgment revealed the **falsehood of Egypt's religion** and the reality that no idol can stand against the living God.

The **religion of Egypt**, marked by **polytheism, magic, spiritism, and idolatry**, stood in stark opposition to the pure worship of **Jehovah**, the one true God. The biblical narrative presents Egypt not as a spiritually advanced society but as a culture steeped in **error, superstition, and rebellion against divine truth**.

The triumph of Jehovah over Egypt's gods through the **miraculous acts performed by Moses and Aaron**, and the **plagues of the Exodus**, serve as enduring testimony to the **sovereignty and holiness of Israel's God**, who alone deserves worship.

Egypt's religious system, despite its grandeur and complexity, brought **no true moral or spiritual uplift** to its people. Instead, it exemplifies the tragic results of turning away from the Creator to serve created things, reinforcing the apostolic declaration:

"They exchanged the truth of God for the lie and worshiped and served the creature rather than the Creator." (Romans 1:25)

Edward D. Andrews

# CHAPTER 7 How Did Animal Worship Reflect the Degrading Idolatry of Egypt?

### Animal Worship

The idolatrous system of ancient **Egyptian religion** reached its most degrading expression in the widespread practice of **animal worship**, a distinctive and notorious feature of Egypt's polytheism throughout its history. The biblical record, consistent with archaeological and historical evidence, affirms that Egypt's religion embraced not only the worship of **false gods** represented in human form but also extended divine status to animals, whether symbolically associated with gods or believed to be direct incarnations of deity.

This perverse veneration of animals exemplifies what the apostle **Paul** described in **Romans 1:22-23**:

"Although they claimed to be wise, they became fools and exchanged the glory of the incorruptible God for images resembling mortal man and birds and animals and creeping things."

Egypt's worship of animals, often portrayed through images combining **human bodies with animal heads** or through the literal reverence of living creatures, illustrates the **spiritual degradation** resulting from turning away from the true God to serve created things. This system not only dishonored the Creator but also dehumanized the worshipers, binding them in superstition and fear of the natural world rather than leading them to truth and holiness.

### Animal-Headed Deities and Divine Incarnations

A striking feature of Egyptian religious iconography is the **depiction of many gods with animal heads**, symbolizing their association with certain aspects of nature or specific animals. This practice reflected the belief that divine power was either represented by or resident within the animal form. Among the most well-known examples are:

- **Horus**: Often depicted with the **head of a falcon**, symbolizing kingship and the sky.
- **Thoth**: Portrayed with the **head of an ibis**, associated with wisdom, writing, and the moon; sometimes represented as an ape.
- **Anubis**: Shown with the **head of a jackal**, regarded as the god of embalming and the protector of graves.
- **Sekhmet**: A goddess with the **head of a lioness**, associated with war and destruction.
- **Sobek**: The crocodile god, linked to fertility and the Nile.
- **Hathor**: Often portrayed with **cow horns and a solar disk**, symbolizing motherhood and love.

These depictions were not merely artistic representations but were rooted in the belief that the **essence or power of the god was directly connected to the animal**, either symbolically or through actual indwelling. Such visualizations permeated Egypt's religious architecture, funerary art, and ritual objects.

This blending of human and animal forms directly contradicted the **biblical view of creation**, where animals were created for mankind's service and dominion, not for worship (Genesis 1:26-28). The exaltation of animals as divine represented an inversion of the proper order established by Jehovah.

### The Cult of Sacred Animals and the Apis Bull

Perhaps the most infamous example of **animal worship in Egypt** was the veneration of the **Apis bull**, regarded as the living embodiment of the god **Osiris**. The Apis bull was not merely symbolic; it was considered an actual **incarnation of divinity**. A living bull, chosen based on specific physical markings believed to indicate divine favor, was kept in a dedicated temple, attended by priests, and honored with elaborate rituals.

At the death of the Apis bull, the animal was accorded an elaborate **funeral procession and burial**, complete with mummification, coffins, and tomb inscriptions akin to royal burials.

Successive Apis bulls were chosen and maintained in this cycle of veneration for centuries.

This practice of **identifying living animals as divine manifestations** extended beyond bulls. Other examples of sacred animal cults in Egypt included:

- **Cats**, associated with the goddess **Bastet**.
- **Crocodiles**, connected with **Sobek**, often kept in temple pools and mummified after death.
- **Baboons**, venerated in connection with **Thoth**.
- **Ibises**, likewise sacred to **Thoth** and mummified in vast numbers.
- **Jackals**, linked to **Anubis**.
- **Kites, falcons, and other birds of prey**, honored as manifestations of various deities.

The archaeological discovery of **animal cemeteries** containing **hundreds of thousands of mummified animals**—cats, crocodiles, ibises, falcons, and others—provides undeniable evidence of the scale and seriousness of animal worship in Egyptian religion. These cemeteries have been excavated at numerous sites, including **Saqqara, Tuna el-Gebel**, and **Crocodilopolis** (modern **Faiyum**).

### Theological Corruption and Moral Degradation

The biblical judgment against **idolatry and animal worship** is not limited to condemning false religious practices as superstitious errors; it exposes these practices as **profound moral corruption and rebellion against the Creator**. By attributing divinity to animals, the Egyptians not only **dishonored Jehovah** but also embraced a worldview that degraded the dignity of both man and beast.

Animals, created by Jehovah for specific roles in His creation, were not intended as objects of veneration. The worship of animals enslaved the Egyptians to **fear, ritual bondage, and spiritual blindness**, reinforcing the superstitions that made them vulnerable to **magic, spiritism, and false hopes**.

# THE EGYPTIAN EMPIRE

In sharp contrast, the law given through **Moses** strictly forbade all forms of **idolatry**, including the making of images of anything in heaven or earth for the purpose of worship (Exodus 20:4-5; Deuteronomy 4:15-19). This commandment stood directly opposed to Egypt's religious system and highlighted the radical difference between **Jehovah's holiness** and the **defilement of Egypt's cultic practices**.

### Egyptian Influence on Israel and the Golden Calf Incident

The allure of Egyptian religious customs did not leave Israel unaffected. After their departure from Egypt, the Israelites fell into idolatry by making a **golden calf** at Mount Sinai (Exodus 32:1-8). This image, described as an **"egel"** (calf), may reflect the influence of **Egyptian bull worship**, particularly the cult of the Apis bull.

The choice of a calf or bull as the form of their idol suggests that even after witnessing Jehovah's power in the plagues and the Exodus, some Israelites still harbored **Egyptian religious associations**. This incident serves as a tragic demonstration of how deeply ingrained the corrupt religious environment of Egypt had become in the minds of those who had lived under its influence.

### Magic, Animal Symbols, and Occult Beliefs

Animal imagery was also central to Egyptian **magic and superstition**. Amulets bearing images of sacred animals were worn for protection, healing, fertility, and success. These charms were often inscribed with magical texts and buried with the dead or tied to the living as talismans.

For example:

- **Scarab beetles**, symbolizing rebirth and regeneration.
- **Cat-shaped amulets**, invoking the favor of **Bastet**.
- **Crocodile-shaped charms**, calling upon **Sobek** for fertility and strength.

Such practices violated the clear prohibitions against **enchantment, sorcery, necromancy, and spiritism** laid down by Jehovah (Deuteronomy 18:10-12). The involvement of animals in these occult rites only intensified the perversion of Egypt's religious life.

**Divine Rebuke Through the Plagues**

Jehovah's **judgment upon Egypt through the plagues** included direct affronts to Egypt's animal cults:

- The **plague upon livestock** (Exodus 9:1-7) struck at the heart of the Apis bull cult and other animal-related deities.
- The **plague of frogs** (Exodus 8:1-6) mocked the goddess **Heket**, often depicted as a frog.
- The **death of the firstborn,** including livestock (Exodus 12:12), demonstrated Jehovah's sovereignty over life, livestock, and the false gods who were powerless to protect their animal representatives.

These acts were not arbitrary punishments; they were deliberate judgments against the idolatrous system that enslaved the Egyptian people in superstition and rebellion.

The **animal worship of Egypt** stands as one of the clearest examples of the **spiritual depravity of polytheism**, reducing the glory of God's creation to objects of reverence and veneration. Egypt's exaltation of animals, whether symbolically represented in deities with animal heads or literally embodied in living creatures like the Apis bull, reflected a profound misunderstanding of the **Creator-creature distinction.**

The biblical record does not idealize Egyptian culture or philosophy. Instead, it exposes the **folly and degradation** of a religious system that worships the creation rather than the Creator. Egypt's animal cults, while elaborate and deeply entrenched, ultimately testified to the **emptiness of idolatry** and the **justice of Jehovah's judgments** against the gods of Egypt.

The triumph of **Jehovah over Egypt's gods**, including those expressed through animal worship, stands as an enduring reminder that only the true God of Israel possesses the power of life, judgment, and deliverance.

# CHAPTER 8 Why Did Moses Insist That Israel's Sacrifices Would Be "Detestable to the Egyptians"?

**The Detestability of Israel's Sacrifices in the Eyes of the Egyptians**

The confrontation between **Moses and Pharaoh** over the release of the Israelites included a specific argument that sheds light on the **religious and cultural tensions** between Israel's worship of **Jehovah** and the idolatrous practices of Egypt. In **Exodus 8:26-27**, Moses, responding to Pharaoh's offer to allow Israel to sacrifice within the land of Egypt, stated:

"It would not be right to do so, for what we would sacrifice to Jehovah our God is detestable to the Egyptians. If we should sacrifice what is detestable to the Egyptians before their eyes, would they not stone us? We must go a three-day journey into the wilderness and sacrifice to Jehovah our God just as he has commanded us."

This insistence on leaving Egypt to offer sacrifices was not mere political maneuvering or negotiation. Rather, it reflected a **fundamental incompatibility between the worship of the true God and the religious worldview of the Egyptians**, especially regarding the **status of certain animals** within Egyptian culture and their role in Egyptian idolatry.

The Hebrew term translated as "detestable" (תּוֹעֵבָה, *toʻevah*) is a strong word used throughout Scripture to describe that which is **abominable, loathsome, or morally repugnant**, often in connection with idolatry and false worship (cf. Deuteronomy 7:25-26; 12:31). Here, it clearly conveys that **the very animals Israel would offer in sacrifice were revered or even deified by the Egyptians**, making such slaughter an offense not only to Egyptian sensibilities but to their religious convictions.

**Animal Deification and the Offense of Sacrifice**

Egyptian religion, as previously discussed, involved **the worship of numerous animals**, either as representations of gods or as the actual incarnations of divine power. Bulls, calves, goats, sheep, rams, crocodiles, ibises, falcons, and cats were among the creatures venerated in various regions of Egypt. Some animals were seen as **sacred symbols**, while others were believed to **embody the spirit of specific deities**.

- The **bull**, for example, was associated with several deities, including the **Apis bull** as a living representation of **Osiris** and at times the sun god **Ra**, who was also symbolized as a **celestial calf**.
- **Rams and goats** were linked to gods such as **Khnum** and **Amun**, both of whom were sometimes depicted with **ram heads**.
- **Sheep** and **cattle** were revered in various cult centers, with specific animals often kept in temples under priestly care.

Given this religious context, the slaughter of these animals—viewed as divine or sacred—would be considered by Egyptians not simply disrespectful but **sacrilegious**, a direct **attack on their gods**. The suggestion of performing such acts "before their eyes" (Exodus 8:26) would provoke violent retaliation, as Moses indicated by the rhetorical question, "Would they not stone us?"

This objection was not speculative. Ancient peoples frequently reacted with hostility toward perceived offenses against their deities. Sacrificing a god's embodiment or symbol would be viewed as an assault on the divine realm itself, making Moses' concern both realistic and strategically wise.

**Israel's Sacrificial System and Its Clash with Egyptian Religion**

The **sacrifices commanded by Jehovah** involved animals commonly associated with Egyptian religious symbolism. Among these were:

- **Bulls and calves**: Used in **burnt offerings and fellowship offerings** (Leviticus 1:5; 3:1).

- **Rams**: Designated for **burnt offerings, peace offerings, and guilt offerings** (Leviticus 8:18-21; 5:15).
- **Goats**: Used for **sin offerings and the Day of Atonement ceremonies** (Leviticus 4:24; 16:5-22).
- **Sheep and lambs**: Central to the **Passover sacrifice**, which marked Israel's deliverance from Egypt (Exodus 12:3-6).

The **Passover lamb**, whose blood marked the Israelites' doorposts during the final plague, may itself have been viewed as **detestable to the Egyptians**, compounding the offense in the eyes of Pharaoh's people. This sacrifice, ordained by Jehovah, was not merely an act of religious duty but a **theological declaration** that the gods of Egypt were **powerless and false**, incapable of defending their symbols from Jehovah's judgment.

Thus, the very practice of Israel's sacrificial system, in obedience to Jehovah's commands, constituted a profound **rejection of Egyptian idolatry** and would have been seen as a direct insult to the religious foundations of Egyptian society.

### Jehovah's Judgment on the "Gods of Egypt"

This backdrop adds weight to Jehovah's declaration in **Exodus 12:12**:

"I will pass through the land of Egypt on that night and strike down every firstborn in the land of Egypt, from man to beast, and I will execute judgment on all the gods of Egypt. I am Jehovah."

The **ten plagues**, culminating in the death of the firstborn, were not arbitrary disasters but deliberate **acts of judgment against Egypt's gods**, exposing their impotence and invalidating their claims to divine power. The Egyptian deities, many represented by animals, could not prevent the slaughter of the firstborn among their sacred creatures or among the people who revered them.

In this way, Israel's sacrifices, particularly if offered within the land of Egypt, would have served as **visible signs of Jehovah's superiority over Egypt's entire religious system**, a reality intolerable to the Egyptians themselves.

### Israel's Contamination with Egyptian Idolatry

The seriousness of Egyptian animal worship is further underscored by the fact that **Israel did not entirely escape its influence** during their long sojourn in Egypt. This contamination became evident:

- When **Joshua**, near the end of the conquest period, exhorted the people:

"Now therefore fear Jehovah and serve him in sincerity and in truth. Put away the gods that your fathers served beyond the River and in Egypt, and serve Jehovah." (Joshua 24:14)

- When **Ezekiel** recounted Jehovah's charge against Israel:

"Throw away each of you the disgusting things of his eyes, and do not defile yourselves with the dungy idols of Egypt. I am Jehovah your God." (Ezekiel 20:7-8)

The persistence of such contamination explains why the **golden calf incident** occurred so readily (Exodus 32:1-8). The form of the calf, resembling Egyptian sacred bulls, reflects the **carryover of Egyptian religious thinking** into the hearts of some Israelites, despite their deliverance from Egypt.

Later history repeated this pattern when **Jeroboam**, after returning from Egypt, established **two golden calves** for worship in **Dan and Bethel** (1 Kings 12:28-29). This decision likely drew on Egyptian models of animal worship, making Israel's apostasy not an isolated act but part of a longer pattern of **idolatrous influence traced back to Egypt**.

### Scriptural Integrity Free from Egyptian Corruption

Notably, despite Israel's exposure to Egyptian religious influence, the **Scriptures written by Moses remain entirely free from contamination by Egyptian idolatry**. The narrative firmly condemns animal worship, polytheism, and magic, consistently upholding **monotheism and the exclusive worship of Jehovah**.

This purity of revelation further underscores that Moses, though raised in Pharaoh's household (Exodus 2:10), was not a product of

Egyptian religious thought. Instead, under divine guidance, he became the instrument for delivering **Jehovah's holy law**, radically distinct from the superstitions and corruptions of Egypt.

Moses' insistence that **Israel's sacrifices would be detestable to the Egyptians** was not mere rhetoric but a reflection of the deep religious divide between the **worship of Jehovah** and the **idolatrous system of Egypt**. The animals selected by Jehovah for sacrifice were often the very creatures revered or deified by the Egyptians. To offer these animals as sacrifices within Egypt would have been perceived as a **direct assault on Egyptian gods**, provoking outrage and violence.

This tension highlights the fundamental incompatibility between the **true worship of Jehovah** and **pagan systems based on idolatry and animal veneration**. The Exodus narrative, through both its theology and historical details, demonstrates the necessity of separating Israel from Egypt's corrupt religious environment to fulfill Jehovah's purposes.

The judgment executed upon Egypt's gods, including the humiliation of their sacred animals, stands as a lasting testimony that **Jehovah alone is God**, and **no false deity, however exalted among men, can stand before His power**.

# CHAPTER 9 What Spiritual and Moral Qualities Were Lacking in Egyptian Religion?

**Spiritual and Moral Qualities Lacking**

The religious system of **ancient Egypt**, though rich in ritual, symbolism, and ceremonial complexity, was fundamentally **devoid of true spiritual depth and moral accountability** as defined by the standards of Jehovah, the one true God. Though the Egyptians built monumental temples, wrote elaborate hymns, and engaged in sophisticated funerary practices, their religion was primarily centered on **external ritualism, superstition, and magical manipulation of the divine**, rather than on genuine moral transformation or heartfelt repentance.

In stark contrast to the **biblical concept of sin, guilt, and the need for repentance before a holy and righteous God**, Egyptian religion offered no true confession of sin in the sense understood by Scripture. There was no recognition of **universal moral accountability before the Creator**, no personal acknowledgment of guilt, and no spiritual longing for reconciliation with God based on divine justice and mercy.

The absence of these essential spiritual and moral qualities reveals the **spiritual bankruptcy of Egyptian religion**, regardless of its cultural achievements or material grandeur. This failure becomes especially apparent when Egypt's religious worldview is compared with the **ethical monotheism of Israel**, as articulated in the inspired writings of **Moses** and the **Hebrew prophets**.

**Negative Confession and the Illusion of Innocence**

One of the clearest illustrations of Egypt's lack of true moral reflection is found in the practice of the so-called **"negative confession"** or **"declaration of innocence"**, preserved in the **Book of the Dead** and other funerary texts. In these rituals, the deceased, when entering the judgment hall of **Osiris**, would recite a list of **sins they claimed not to have committed**, asserting innocence rather than confessing guilt.

As summarized by the **Encyclopædia Britannica (1959, Vol. 8, p. 56)**:

"When [the Egyptian] confessed he did not say 'I am guilty'; he said 'I am not guilty.' His confession was negative, and the onus probandi [the burden of proof] lay on his judges, who, according to the funerary papyri, always gave the verdict in his favour—or at any rate it was hoped and expected that they would do so."

This approach reveals a profound difference between **Egyptian religious thought** and the **biblical doctrine of sin**. The biblical view recognizes the **universal sinfulness of mankind** (Romans 3:23) and the necessity of **humble confession and repentance** before God. David's heartfelt plea in **Psalm 51:1-5** stands in direct opposition to the Egyptian concept:

"Have mercy on me, O God, according to your loyal love; according to your great compassion wipe out my transgressions. Thoroughly wash me from my error, and cleanse me from my sin. For I am well aware of my transgressions, and my sin is always before me. Against you, you above all, I have sinned, and what is bad in your eyes I have done."

The **negative confession** of the Egyptians thus reflects **self-justification**, presumption of innocence, and ritualistic expectation of favorable judgment, with no genuine sense of **contrition or moral responsibility**. It reduces divine judgment to a mere formality, a ceremonial process easily manipulated by proper words and magical spells.

### Ritualism Over Righteousness

Egyptian religion prioritized **ceremonial observance and magical formulas** over any meaningful pursuit of moral virtue. Worship was predominantly **external and mechanical**, focusing on rituals intended to **placate or manipulate deities** rather than on any interior transformation of character.

The emphasis on **"spells" and "incantations"** in Egyptian funerary literature underscores this approach. These texts were designed to equip the deceased with the necessary verbal formulas to navigate the dangers of the afterlife successfully. Salvation, in this system, was not based on a right relationship with God but on **proper ritual performance** and **magical knowledge**.

Such practices are repeatedly condemned in Scripture, where Jehovah rejects **mechanical ritualism without righteousness** (Isaiah 1:11-17; Amos 5:21-24). True worship, according to the Bible, demands not empty ceremonies but **obedience, justice, mercy, and humility** before God (Micah 6:6-8).

The Egyptian focus on **magical effectiveness rather than moral integrity** left the system spiritually barren, offering no real solution for sin or hope of redemption. Egyptian religion could only promise success in the afterlife through correct spells, not through the grace and forgiveness of a righteous God.

### The False Notion of Monotheism Under Akhenaton

Some modern scholars have suggested that Egypt flirted with a form of **monotheism** during the reigns of **Amenhotep III** and particularly **Amenhotep IV (Akhenaton)**, who elevated the **sun-disk Aton** as the supreme, and at times nearly exclusive, object of worship. However, this so-called "monotheism" was neither pure nor true in the biblical sense:

- The **Pharaoh himself continued to be regarded as divine**, maintaining the blasphemous concept of **divine kingship**.

- The hymns to Aton, though praising the sun-disk for its life-giving energy, **lacked ethical content** and spiritual aspiration. There was no call for repentance, justice, or personal holiness—only poetic admiration for the warmth and light of the sun.

This stands in stark contrast to the **biblical revelation of Jehovah**, who not only creates and sustains the universe but also demands righteousness, judges sin, and offers mercy to the penitent.

Jehovah is not merely a source of life; He is the **holy Lawgiver and Redeemer**, actively involved in the moral order of His creation.

Any suggestion that **Moses' monotheism derived from Egyptian Atonism** is entirely without foundation. Moses' writings present a **consistent ethical monotheism** grounded in divine revelation, not in Egyptian religious thought. Nowhere in the Egyptian system, even under Akhenaton, is there anything resembling the **covenantal relationship** between God and His people, the **moral law** of Sinai, or the **redemptive plan of atonement** through sacrifice foreshadowing the work of Christ.

### Egyptian Religion as Spiritually Barren

The lack of **spiritual and moral substance** in Egyptian religion is evident not only in its failure to address human sin but also in its underlying **materialistic focus**. The Egyptians sought primarily **material blessings**, such as fertility, agricultural prosperity, and political stability. The deities were expected to **provide tangible benefits**, not to call the people to ethical accountability.

The religious obligations of the people were largely passive. As long as the **priests performed the correct rituals,** and as long as the people participated in festivals and processions, divine favor was assumed. This transactional view of religion—offering worship for the sake of material gain—reveals a system centered on **self-interest, not spiritual devotion.**

Even Egypt's veneration of the dead, including elaborate mummification and tomb construction, was driven not by spiritual yearning but by the desire to **secure a favorable afterlife through preservation of the body and magical protection**, rather than through any transformation of the soul.

This stands in opposition to the biblical message that **life, death, and judgment belong to Jehovah alone**, and that true worship involves **spirit and truth** (John 4:23-24), not ritual and manipulation.

### Moral Vacuum and Israel's Distinctiveness

The contrast between **Egyptian religion** and the **faith of Israel** becomes even clearer when the ethical content of the **Law of Moses** is considered. The Torah lays out **clear moral directives** governing every aspect of life—personal behavior, social justice, sexual ethics, honest commerce, compassion for the poor, and reverence for the sanctity of life.

Egyptian religion, by contrast, offered **no binding moral code with divine authority,** no covenant relationship based on love and obedience, and no assurance of forgiveness through grace. The lack of spiritual and moral qualities in Egypt's religious system explains why Jehovah commanded Israel to **remain separate from the religious practices of Egypt** and warned repeatedly against returning to Egypt either physically or spiritually (Deuteronomy 17:16; Joshua 24:14).

Though Israel was exposed to Egyptian idolatry during their **two centuries of sojourning** there, the inspired Scriptures written by **Moses** remained **completely free of Egyptian contamination**, affirming the **uniqueness of Israel's faith** and the reality of **divine revelation** from Jehovah alone.

The **religion of ancient Egypt**, despite its ceremonial complexity and artistic grandeur, was fundamentally **devoid of spiritual vitality and moral substance**. Its negative confession, ritualism, and reliance on magic could neither cleanse sin nor cultivate righteousness. In place of heartfelt repentance and ethical accountability, Egyptian religion offered hollow formulas and mechanical observances.

The absence of genuine moral conviction, coupled with a transactional approach to the divine, left Egypt spiritually barren. By contrast, the faith of Israel, as revealed through Moses, presented a **holy, just, and merciful God**, calling His people to **love, obedience, and repentance**, not mere ritual performance.

This radical difference between Egypt's empty ceremonialism and Israel's revealed religion confirms the uniqueness of **biblical monotheism** and the futility of any attempt to trace Israel's worship to Egyptian religious ideas. Jehovah alone is God, and His ways are righteous and true.

# CHAPTER 10 What Were the Egyptian Beliefs About the Dead, and How Did They Contrast with Biblical Truth?

### Beliefs About the Dead

A central feature of **ancient Egyptian religion**—arguably its most distinctive and defining characteristic—was its **obsessive concern for the dead and the afterlife**. More than any other aspect of their worship, the Egyptians devoted extraordinary resources, labor, and ritual to securing the well-being of the deceased in what they regarded as **"the next life."** This preoccupation shaped Egypt's monumental architecture, religious literature, and burial customs. It produced one of the most elaborate systems of funerary practices known in the ancient world, including **mummification, tomb construction, grave goods provision,** and **magical inscriptions** intended to ensure the soul's survival and comfort after death.

At the heart of this belief system was the **doctrine of the immortal soul and its transmigration**, along with the conviction that the dead required **physical preservation and material goods** to enjoy happiness and security in the afterlife. Yet, despite these efforts, the Egyptian worldview was fundamentally materialistic, magical, and devoid of true spiritual hope. Their beliefs stood in stark contrast to the **biblical doctrine of death as a state of unconsciousness** (Ecclesiastes 9:5-6, 10) and resurrection as the only means of restoration to life (Job 14:13-15; Daniel 12:2).

### The Doctrine of the Immortal Soul and Body Preservation

The Egyptians held that each person possessed multiple spiritual components, including the **ka** (life force), **ba** (personality or soul), and **akh** (the transfigured spirit). According to Egyptian thought, the **ka** required sustenance in the form of food and drink offerings, while the **ba** was believed to roam freely, capable of leaving the tomb but needing to return periodically to the body. The **akh** represented the effective spiritual entity that would survive death after the proper rituals were observed.

Integral to this belief was the **notion of the soul's immortality**—an idea that, while prominent in Egyptian theology, is explicitly rejected by Scripture, which teaches that **man is a soul (nephesh)**, not that he possesses an inherently immortal soul (Genesis 2:7). The Bible consistently affirms that **the soul that sins will die** (Ezekiel 18:4, 20), and the only hope for future life lies in **resurrection, not reincarnation or transmigration**.

Nevertheless, the Egyptians believed that in order for the **ba** to return to the body and for the individual to function effectively in the afterlife, the **corpse had to be physically preserved**. This conviction drove the practice of **mummification**, an elaborate embalming process aimed at preventing decay and ensuring the body remained a viable "vessel" for the soul.

The significance placed on body preservation is illustrated in the case of **Jacob and Joseph**, whose embalming is recorded in **Genesis 50:2-3, 26**. However, the **embalming of Jacob** served a practical purpose—to preserve his body for transport to the burial site in the Promised Land (Genesis 50:5-13)—in harmony with his faith in Jehovah's promises. **Joseph's embalming**, while performed by Egyptians, likely reflected cultural practices of respect for a high official but did not signify acceptance of Egyptian religious beliefs by Joseph or his family (Genesis 50:24-26).

Thus, the biblical record clearly distinguishes between **Egyptian superstition** and the **faith of the patriarchs**, who understood death as a sleep awaiting resurrection (Job 14:14-15; Hebrews 11:22), not as continued conscious existence or return of the soul.

**Tombs, Grave Goods, and the "Book of the Dead"**

Egyptian tombs were constructed as **"eternal houses"** for the dead, meant to serve as dwelling places for the soul. The grandest of these were the **pyramids**, colossal monuments built primarily during the **Old Kingdom** period as burial chambers for the pharaohs, whom the Egyptians regarded as divine. Later, rock-cut tombs in the **Valley** of the Kings and elsewhere continued this tradition of monumental burial, though on a different architectural scale.

Within these tombs, the Egyptians placed an abundance of **grave goods**—furniture, jewelry, clothing, weapons, tools, cosmetics, food supplies, and even the mummified remains of animals—intended to provide for the deceased's needs in the afterlife. The concept was entirely materialistic: the dead were believed to require **physical objects** to enjoy comfort and protection.

Perhaps most revealing of the spiritual emptiness of this system were the **magical texts** placed alongside the deceased, including the famous **"Book of the Dead"** (known in Egyptian as the "Book of Going Forth by Day"). This collection of **spells, prayers, and incantations** was designed to help the soul navigate the perils of the underworld, confront hostile spirits, and gain favorable judgment from the gods.

These writings reflect a worldview focused on **manipulation of spiritual forces through magical knowledge**, not on humble submission to a righteous Creator. The spells often include instructions for deceiving or appeasing deities, securing safe passage past obstacles, and ensuring the correct answers in the afterlife's "trial by judgment."

Yet, despite these elaborate precautions, Egypt's tombs could not guarantee safety. Archaeological excavations have revealed that **almost all major tombs were eventually plundered** by human thieves, and the "magical protections" inscribed upon their walls and amulets proved **powerless to prevent desecration**.

The stark contrast between Egypt's futile efforts to secure the dead and the **biblical hope of resurrection by Jehovah's power** could not be greater. Whereas Egyptian belief sought to **preserve the dead through human effort and magic**, Scripture teaches that the dead remain unconscious, without knowledge or activity, awaiting the **resurrection at God's appointed time** (Ecclesiastes 9:5-6, 10; John 5:28-29).

**The Judgment Scene and the Scales of Ma'at**

Egyptian funerary texts often depict a **judgment scene** where the deceased's heart is weighed against the feather of **Ma'at**, the goddess of truth and justice. If the heart balanced favorably, the deceased was admitted to the blessed afterlife. If not, the heart would be devoured by **Ammit**, a fearsome hybrid creature.

However, as noted in scholarly analysis, this judgment was typically skewed toward leniency. The **negative confession**, in which the deceased denied wrongdoing rather than admitting guilt, placed the burden on the judges to prove otherwise—a process manipulated by **magical spells** and the expectation of favorable outcomes.

This superficial approach to moral judgment, based on **ritual formulas rather than true repentance**, contrasts sharply with the biblical teaching that **Jehovah judges the heart and requires righteousness, justice, and mercy** (Psalm 7:9; Jeremiah 17:10; Micah 6:8). Divine judgment in Scripture is based not on ritual performance but on the reality of a person's relationship with God and obedience to His commandments.

### Reincarnation, Transmigration, and Immortality of the Soul

The Egyptians believed not only in an immortal soul but also in **reincarnation** or **transmigration**, the idea that the soul could pass through various stages or forms of existence. This doctrine, however, lacks any basis in Scripture. The Bible teaches that death is the **end of conscious existence** and that the hope for future life rests solely in the **resurrection by God's power** (Psalm 146:3-4; Job 14:14-15; John 11:23-26).

By contrast, Egypt's belief system sought to secure immortality through **mummification, tomb preparation, and magical intervention**, all of which proved incapable of preventing either physical decay or spiritual corruption.

### The Failure of Egyptian Hope Versus the Certainty of Jehovah's Promise

Despite their monumental efforts, the Egyptians' hope for the afterlife was built on **fragile human contrivance**—rituals, spells, material provisions, and superstition. Their trust in the preservation of the body and the manipulation of spiritual forces through magic stands in stark opposition to the **biblical doctrine of resurrection**, where life is restored solely by the **creative power of Jehovah**, not by human action (Isaiah 26:19; 1 Corinthians 15:20-22).

The patriarchs—**Abraham, Isaac, Jacob, and Joseph**—knew nothing of such superstitious practices. Instead, they placed their hope in the **promises of God**, desiring burial in the land of promise as a testimony to their faith in Jehovah's future fulfillment (Genesis 49:29-32; Hebrews 11:13-16).

The embalming of **Jacob and Joseph**, recorded in **Genesis 50**, must be understood in this light: as **practical measures within an Egyptian context**, not as theological endorsement of Egyptian beliefs about the dead.

The **beliefs of the Egyptians about the dead**, centered on **immortal soul doctrine, body preservation, magical spells, and grave goods**, reflect a system devoid of true spiritual understanding. Their elaborate rituals, while culturally impressive, were built on a foundation of **false theology and empty superstition**, offering no real hope for deliverance from death.

The Scriptures stand in clear opposition to these beliefs, affirming that **death is a state of unconsciousness**, that **the soul is not immortal**, and that only **Jehovah holds the power of life and resurrection**. The Egyptian hope was misplaced, and their magnificent tombs, now looted and empty, serve as enduring monuments to the futility of trusting in human schemes rather than in the **living God who raises the dead.**

# CHAPTER 11 What Was Egyptian Life and Culture Like in the Biblical Period?

### Egyptian Life and Culture

The cultural achievements of **ancient Egypt** have long captivated historians and archaeologists, who often portray Egypt as the earliest and most sophisticated of human civilizations. Monumental architecture, complex social organization, and technological skill have contributed to the perception of Egypt as a forerunner in human progress. However, when Egypt's cultural development is carefully examined through the lens of both **Scripture and archaeology**, it becomes evident that while Egypt attained remarkable material advancements, its society was deeply shaped by **idolatry, superstition, and moral corruption**, limiting its true value as a source of spiritual insight.

Scripture does not deny Egypt's technical skill or organizational capabilities. Indeed, **Moses**, raised in Pharaoh's house, was "instructed in all the wisdom of the Egyptians" (Acts 7:22). Yet, it was not Egyptian knowledge, but Jehovah's revelation, that formed the basis for true understanding of life, justice, and worship. This section explores the life and culture of Egypt, showing how its practices align with the biblical record and how they stand in contrast to the values of God's covenant people.

### Egypt and the Cradle of Civilization

While older scholarship often portrayed Egypt as the **origin of civilization**, more recent evidence affirms that **Mesopotamia**, not Egypt, holds the rightful place as the earliest center of human development following the dispersion at **Babel** (Genesis 11:8-9). Egypt's adoption of certain innovations—including the **wheel**, elements of **pictographic writing**, and architectural techniques—likely reflect influence from Mesopotamian culture. This corresponds with the biblical record of early postdiluvian human activity radiating outward from the plains of **Shinar**.

Egypt's achievements, though impressive, were not the pioneering breakthroughs of isolated genius but rather the products of cultural borrowing and adaptation, consistent with the **Bible's genealogical and historical framework.**

### Architectural Achievement and Monumental Construction

Egypt's most famous architectural feats, especially the **pyramids of Giza**, constructed during the **Fourth Dynasty**, remain among the most iconic symbols of the ancient world. The **Great Pyramid of Khufu (Cheops)**, covering approximately **13 acres** and originally standing **450 feet high**, involved the placement of **2.3 million limestone blocks,** each weighing an average of **2.3 metric tons**. Such precision in construction speaks to **advanced mathematical knowledge**, including geometry and measurement techniques.

Colossal temple complexes such as **Karnak at Thebes** (biblical **No**, Jeremiah 46:25; Ezekiel 30:14-16) represent additional architectural accomplishments, with massive columns, obelisks, and stone carvings dedicated to Egypt's pantheon of gods.

While these works reflect notable human ingenuity, their purpose was rooted in the **promotion of false worship**, glorifying the Pharaohs as divine and perpetuating the superstitious worldview that dominated Egyptian life.

### Education and Literacy

Education in Egypt centered around **scribal schools**, primarily run by **priests**. Literacy was not widespread but was cultivated among the elite, particularly those who served in administrative roles. Egyptian scribes mastered **hieroglyphic writing**, **hieratic script**, and later **demotic**, as well as **Aramaic cuneiform**, the diplomatic language of the region in the **second millennium B.C.E.** Correspondence between Egyptian officials and rulers in **Syria-Palestine**—such as the **Amarna Letters**—illustrates this bilingual competency.

The **mathematical skill** necessary for pyramid construction and surveying, as well as administrative accounting, suggests an advanced understanding of practical arithmetic and geometry. However, as the biblical record asserts, **true wisdom does not lie in technical skill**

**alone** (Proverbs 1:7), and Egypt's so-called wisdom was polluted by its reliance on **magic, superstition, and idolatry**.

Moses' exposure to this "wisdom of the Egyptians" (Acts 7:22) did not shape the theological truths he delivered through the Law. Rather, **Jehovah's direct revelation** stands in deliberate contrast to Egyptian learning, ensuring that the inspired Scriptures are free from contamination by Egyptian religious error.

**Government, Law, and Social Structure**

Egyptian government was an **absolute monarchy**, with **Pharaoh regarded as divine**, the human son of **Ra** and the intermediary between gods and people. Pharaoh exercised authority through **ministers, provincial governors (nomarchs), and feudal chiefs**, whose power at times rivaled that of the central throne, especially during periods of dynastic weakness.

The biblical references to the **"kings of Egypt"** (plural) may reflect these regional rulers who operated as virtual kings within their domains (2 Kings 7:6; Jeremiah 46:25). Egypt's military governance extended through conquest into **Nubia (Cush)** and at times into **Phoenicia**, with viceroys appointed over these regions.

No systematic **written code of law** from Egypt has survived, and evidence suggests that law was largely **arbitrary, subject to the decrees of Pharaoh**. The Pharaoh's edicts, such as the order to drown Israelite male infants (Exodus 1:22) or to impose harsh labor quotas (Exodus 5:6-18), reflect this autocratic legal structure.

Taxation, often exacted in **produce, livestock, and labor**, began significantly during **Joseph's administration**, when the land of Egypt (except that of the priests) came under Pharaoh's ownership (Genesis 47:20-26). Labor conscription for government projects, including construction and military service, was a common feature of Egyptian economic control.

Punishments for crimes were severe, including **mutilation (such as cutting off the nose), beatings, exile to mines, imprisonment**, and **execution by beheading** (Genesis 39:20; 40:1-3, 16-22). Justice, as in many ancient cultures, was not grounded in consistent legal principles but in **the will of the ruler and the social hierarchy**.

### Social Customs: Marriage, Medicine, and Daily Life

Egyptian marriage customs permitted **polygamy** and even **incestuous unions**, including **brother-sister marriages** among royalty. Such practices were considered fitting for Pharaohs who claimed divine status, asserting that no other women were sufficiently "holy" to bear their offspring. This cultural tolerance for incest starkly contrasts with the **prohibitions of the Mosaic Law** (Leviticus 18:3, 6-16), where Jehovah explicitly commands Israel **not to imitate the moral degeneracy of Egypt or Canaan**.

Egyptian medicine combined **practical knowledge of anatomy** with **deep-rooted superstition and magic**. While some surgical techniques and herbal remedies were employed, much of Egyptian medical practice involved **spells, incantations, and ingredients like mouse blood, excrement, and urine**. Magical thinking dominated their approach to healing, including efforts to "drive out demons" through disgusting mixtures intended to repel evil spirits.

The diseases endemic to Egypt—including **dysentery, plague, elephantiasis, smallpox, and ophthalmia**—highlight the failure of these practices. Jehovah's Law, in contrast, instituted **hygienic measures** that dramatically reduced the spread of disease (Deuteronomy 7:15; 28:27, 58-60; Leviticus 11:32-40), demonstrating divine wisdom far superior to Egyptian medicine.

### Economy, Industry, and Trade

Egypt's economy relied on **agriculture**, facilitated by the **annual flooding of the Nile**, along with a wide variety of crafts and industries. Egyptian artisans practiced **pottery making, metalworking, weaving, glass manufacturing, jewelry production, and stone carving** (Isaiah 19:1, 9-10; Job 28:17). By the **mid-second millennium B.C.E.**, Egypt had become a center for **glassmaking**, producing colored glass beads, vessels, and inlays.

Trade extended through **caravans into Africa** and by **ships across the Red Sea** and the **eastern Mediterranean**. The Nile remained the principal transportation artery, with **sailing vessels and barges** moving goods upstream and downstream, aided by the prevailing winds and the river's current.

### Domestic Life and Clothing

Egyptian homes ranged from **simple huts of the poor** to **villas of the wealthy**, often designed around **open courtyards** where much daily activity, including **cooking and food preparation**, took place (compare Exodus 8:3, 13). Wealthier homes featured **gardens, orchards, and pools**. Furniture ranged from basic stools to ornate couches and carved chairs.

Egyptian diets typically consisted of **barley bread, vegetables, fish, and beer** as the common drink. Meat was reserved for the affluent, while the lower classes relied on more modest fare (Numbers 11:5; Exodus 16:3).

Clothing was generally **simple and functional**: men often wore **pleated kilts or aprons**, while women wore **close-fitting linen garments with shoulder straps**. Footwear was typically absent, contributing to the prevalence of foot-related diseases. Use of **cosmetics and personal grooming**—including shaving the head and face—was widespread among both men and women (Genesis 41:14).

### Military Power and Warfare

Egypt's military employed **bows and arrows, spears, maces, axes, and daggers**, with **horse-drawn chariots** playing a critical role in warfare. Chariots became especially prominent in **New Kingdom military campaigns**, as reflected in biblical accounts (Exodus 14:6-28). Armor and helmets were later additions to Egyptian military equipment.

The **prophecy of Jeremiah (46:2-4)** accurately describes Egyptian military practices in the **seventh century B.C.E.**, consistent with archaeological findings. Egypt's armies included both **conscripts from the native population** and **mercenaries from other nations**, often used to bolster military campaigns.

The culture of **ancient Egypt**, while outwardly impressive in its art, architecture, and organization, was marked by **spiritual**

**emptiness, moral corruption, and superstition.** Its technological skill and administrative sophistication could not compensate for its **idolatry, injustice, and false religion**. Egyptian life and culture serve as a vivid illustration of human achievement divorced from divine truth—a civilization rich in material greatness but impoverished in spiritual substance.

The biblical narrative faithfully reflects the historical realities of Egyptian life while affirming the **superiority of Jehovah's ways** in law, morality, worship, and understanding of life itself.

# CHAPTER 12 What Does the Bible Reveal About Abraham's Visit to Egypt?

**Abraham's Visit**

The account of **Abraham's journey into Egypt**, recorded in **Genesis 12:10-20**, represents the first significant intersection between the biblical patriarchs and the Egyptian world. This event is not merely a passing detail in the narrative of Abraham's life but is deeply informative about the cultural, economic, and geopolitical environment of Egypt during the early second millennium B.C.E. Moreover, it provides a vivid example of how Jehovah's covenant purposes were preserved in the face of human failure and foreign power.

Abraham's experience in Egypt offers critical insight into the **moral character of Egyptian leadership**, the pervasive instability caused by famine in the ancient Near East, and the providential safeguarding of the **promised seed through divine intervention**. The historical setting, though briefly described, is in perfect harmony with what is known about Egypt's political conditions, social customs, and economic strength at the time.

**The Context of the Journey: Famine and Egypt's Economic Role**

The biblical text introduces Abraham's descent into Egypt as a response to **severe famine in Canaan**:

"A famine arose in the land, and Abram went down into Egypt to reside there for a while, because the famine was severe." (Genesis 12:10)

The occurrence of famine in **Canaan** is historically credible, as the **southern Levant** depended heavily on seasonal rainfall for agriculture. Periodic droughts and crop failures would have made the Nile-fed fields of Egypt, with their more reliable irrigation systems, a natural destination for relief seekers.

# THE EGYPTIAN EMPIRE

Egypt's **dependence on the Nile and its sophisticated irrigation methods**, as discussed in previous sections, made it a **regional granary** and a refuge for those in surrounding lands during times of scarcity. This feature of Egyptian agriculture, confirmed by archaeological evidence and Egyptian records, fully aligns with the biblical depiction of Egypt as a place where food could still be secured while famine gripped neighboring regions.

Such economic realities explain why **Abraham** chose Egypt as his destination. However, the text does not portray this choice as a divinely sanctioned decision. Rather, the episode reveals **Abraham's human vulnerability**, exposing the patriarch's lapse into fear-driven calculation rather than faith-based reliance on Jehovah's protection.

**Abraham's Fear and the Supposed Deception Regarding Sarah**

Upon nearing Egypt, Abraham voiced his concern regarding the safety of both himself and his wife **Sarah**, stating:

"Please say you are my sister, so that it may go well with me on account of you, and my life will be spared because of you." (Genesis 12:13)

This request was rooted in the **cultural customs of Egypt and the ancient Near East**, where the taking of a woman into a ruler's harem was not uncommon if her husband could be conveniently eliminated. By claiming Sarah as his sister, Abraham sought to avoid potential harm, although this was a **half-truth**, since Sarah was indeed his half-sister (Genesis 20:12).

According to the Book of Genesis, Sarah was Abraham's half-sister. In Genesis 20:12, Abraham describes her as "my father's daughter, but not my mother's," meaning they shared the same father but different mothers. This is a key point in the narrative, as it explains why Abraham initially presented Sarah as his sister to King Abimelech.

This incident provides valuable historical insight into the **practice of royal acquisition of foreign women**, a well-attested phenomenon in Egyptian history. Pharaohs and high officials routinely expanded their harems through the taking of beautiful women from abroad, sometimes under the pretense of diplomacy, at other times by force. The narrative suggests that Sarah's beauty was sufficient to attract the attention of **Pharaoh's officials**, who then recommended her for the royal household (Genesis 12:14-15).

### Understanding Abraham's Actions in Egypt and Gerar

The account of Abraham presenting Sarah as his sister in both Egypt (Genesis 12:10–20) and Gerar (Genesis 20:1–18) has often raised the question of whether he was engaging in deception. If lying is condemned by God (Exodus 20:16), how could Abraham, a man counted as righteous and faithful (Genesis 15:6), engage in such behavior and still receive divine blessings? To understand this, it is necessary to examine the biblical definition of lying, the cultural background of Abraham's actions, and the theological implications of these events.

### Was Abraham's Statement a Lie?

A lie is generally understood as an intentional falsehood designed to deceive or harm. However, Abraham's statement about Sarah was technically true—Sarah was indeed his half-sister. In Genesis 20:12, Abraham clarifies, "Besides, she is indeed my sister, the daughter of my father though not the daughter of my mother, and she became my wife." Thus, his statement was not entirely false but was an omission of crucial information that could have prevented potential trouble.

While withholding truth can sometimes be deceptive, the biblical standard for lying primarily condemns malicious falsehood—statements intended to harm others. Abraham's actions appear to stem from fear rather than malicious intent. He anticipated that the rulers of these foreign lands might kill him to take Sarah as their own (Genesis 12:12), a practice that was not uncommon in ancient times. Given that Sarah was very beautiful (Genesis 12:11, 20:2), Abraham was genuinely concerned for his life.

### Withholding Information from Those Who Do Not Deserve It

Throughout the Bible, withholding information from those who would use it for evil purposes is not equated with sinful deception.

Jesus himself demonstrated this principle when he avoided direct answers to certain religious leaders who sought to trap him (Matthew 21:23–27; John 7:3–10). He also instructed his followers, "Do not give dogs what is holy, and do not throw your pearls before pigs, lest they trample them underfoot and turn to attack you" (Matthew 7:6). This shows that there are situations where full disclosure is not required, especially when dealing with hostile individuals.

The Bible records other instances where individuals withheld information for self-preservation or to protect others:

- **Isaac** repeated Abraham's actions and presented Rebekah as his sister to King Abimelech (Genesis 26:6–11).
- **Rahab** hid the Israelite spies and misled the men of Jericho (Joshua 2:1–6). James 2:25 commends Rahab for her faith, demonstrating that her actions were not counted against her.
- **Elisha** misled the Aramean army to protect Israel (2 Kings 6:19–23).

These examples indicate that in certain extreme situations, withholding information from those with malicious intent was acceptable.

**Pharaoh's Guilt and Divine Intervention**

Abraham's deception, though intended for self-preservation, placed both him and Sarah in a morally compromising position. However, the biblical record emphasizes that Jehovah did not allow Abraham's faithlessness to derail His covenant purposes. Instead, **Jehovah intervened directly**:

"But Jehovah struck Pharaoh and his household with severe plagues because of Sarai, Abram's wife." (Genesis 12:17)

The exact nature of these plagues is not specified, but the plural term implies a series of calamities, likely affecting Pharaoh's household and possibly the fertility or health of those involved. The immediate effectiveness of these plagues in compelling Pharaoh to release Sarah suggests that the divine punishment was unmistakable.

It is significant that **Pharaoh, though an idolatrous ruler**, quickly recognized his guilt and questioned Abraham sharply:

"What have you done to me? Why did you not tell me that she was your wife? Why did you say, 'She is my sister,' so that I was about to take her as my wife? Now here is your wife. Take her and go!" (Genesis 12:18-19)

The moral irony is striking: the pagan Pharaoh appears more ethically upright in this situation than Abraham, who failed to trust Jehovah fully. Yet this account serves to magnify Jehovah's **sovereign control and faithfulness**, demonstrating that even human error could not thwart His purpose to preserve the promised line through which the Messiah would eventually come.

**The Political Environment of Egypt During Abraham's Visit**

Although the biblical text does not name the specific Pharaoh involved, the timing of Abraham's journey (circa **1943 B.C.E.**) situates this event within what scholars designate as the **Middle Kingdom period of Egyptian history** (circa 2055–1650 B.C.E.). This period was characterized by a relatively **strong central government**, flourishing trade, and ongoing construction projects, though Egypt's engagement with Asiatic populations was limited compared to the later **Hyksos period**.

The absence of a Pharaoh's personal name in the account is consistent with the **biblical focus on theological, not dynastic, history**. Scripture emphasizes Pharaoh as a representative of Egypt's power structure rather than as an individual whose personal achievements are of spiritual significance. This omission also underscores that Egypt's greatness was **irrelevant to the outworking of Jehovah's purpose**, which centered on Abraham and his descendants.

Egyptian royal policy toward foreigners, including **Semitic peoples**, is well documented in later periods, particularly during the Hyksos occupation. While direct evidence from the Middle Kingdom is limited regarding foreign women in royal harems, parallels in subsequent periods validate the cultural plausibility of such a practice during Abraham's time.

### Material Gain from Egypt

Despite Abraham's failure, Jehovah ensured that Abraham emerged from Egypt **protected and materially enriched**:

"Pharaoh then gave his men orders concerning him, and they sent him away with his wife and all that he had." (Genesis 12:20)

Earlier, the text notes that Pharaoh had treated Abraham well for Sarah's sake:

"And he had sheep, cattle, male donkeys, male and female servants, female donkeys, and camels." (Genesis 12:16)

This accumulation of wealth would later contribute to Abraham's growing household and economic status (Genesis 13:2). While these material gains may have been intended as bride-price gifts from Pharaoh, they became part of Abraham's holdings, ultimately supporting the fulfillment of God's promise to bless Abraham (Genesis 12:2-3).

Yet the account carefully avoids any suggestion that such prosperity justified Abraham's deception. Rather, it underscores the **unmerited favor of Jehovah**, who safeguarded His promise despite Abraham's failure.

### Theological Significance of Abraham's Visit to Egypt

The episode of Abraham in Egypt serves several critical theological purposes in the unfolding narrative of Genesis:

1. It illustrates the **fragility of human faith** when confronted with danger, yet highlights Jehovah's **unbreakable covenant faithfulness**.

2. It anticipates future interactions between **Abraham's descendants and Egypt**, including the enslavement of Israel and the Exodus deliverance.

3. It establishes a pattern of **divine protection for the seed of promise**, regardless of foreign threats or the schemes of human rulers.

4. It contrasts the **moral bankruptcy of human solutions** with the **sovereign power of God**, who alone ensures the success of His redemptive plan.

This early encounter with Egypt foreshadows the later **plagues upon Pharaoh during the Exodus** (Exodus 7–12), where once again Jehovah would strike Egypt to protect His people and make His name known. The connection between these events reveals that Jehovah's dealings with Egypt, whether in Abraham's time or in Moses', were always directed toward the **vindication of His name and the safeguarding of His covenant people**.

Abraham's visit to Egypt, while brief, holds profound significance in the biblical account. It highlights the **danger of relying on human cunning instead of divine guidance**, the moral pitfalls of foreign alliances, and the unwavering faithfulness of Jehovah to protect the line of promise. The cultural practices of Egypt—its royal acquisition of women, its power structures, and its material wealth—provide a credible historical backdrop for the narrative, yet they also stand as a contrast to the spiritual values Jehovah would later instill in Israel through His Law.

This episode serves as an early demonstration that **no earthly power, no matter how great, can frustrate the purposes of the sovereign God of heaven and earth.**

# CHAPTER 13 What Role Did Joseph Play in Egypt, and How Did His Rise Demonstrate Jehovah's Sovereign Purpose?

### Joseph in Egypt

The account of **Joseph in Egypt**, spanning **Genesis 37 through 50**, presents one of the most remarkable and providential narratives in Scripture. It records the journey of **Joseph**, sold by his own brothers into slavery, rising by God's providence to the position of **second in command over Egypt**, directly under Pharaoh. This episode not only reveals the operation of **Jehovah's sovereignty through human history**, but it also provides one of the Bible's most detailed pictures of Egyptian society during the **Middle Kingdom period** (circa 2055–1650 B.C.E.), offering valuable historical insights consistent with the cultural realities of that time.

The experience of Joseph and his role in Egypt further fulfills Jehovah's earlier statement to **Abraham**:

"Know for certain that your descendants will be foreigners in a land not theirs, and they will have to serve the people there, and these will afflict them for 400 years." (Genesis 15:13)

While the **enslavement proper** began later under a Pharaoh who "did not know Joseph" (Exodus 1:8), Joseph's account begins the process of **Israelite presence in Egypt**, leading eventually to their multiplication into a nation.

### Joseph's Enslavement and Egypt's Slave Trade

After his brothers, driven by envy and hatred, sold him to **Ishmaelite traders**, Joseph was brought into Egypt, where he was sold to **Potiphar**, "an officer of Pharaoh, the chief of the guard" (Genesis 37:28, 36; 39:1). This aligns well with what is known of **slave trading routes** between the Levant and Egypt during the Middle

Kingdom. Semitic slaves from **Canaanite regions** are attested in Egyptian records, sometimes referred to as **Asiatics** (Aamu).

The Egyptian society of that period, with its structured hierarchy and emphasis on **administrative control**, often employed slaves in household service, military roles, or construction projects. Joseph's initial placement in Potiphar's house matches this cultural background.

### Joseph's Integrity and False Accusation

While serving in Potiphar's house, Joseph quickly rose to a position of responsibility due to his **trustworthiness and skill**. The Bible records:

"Jehovah was with Joseph, and he became successful… His master saw that Jehovah was with him." (Genesis 39:2-3)

However, **Potiphar's wife** attempted to seduce him, and upon his refusal, falsely accused him of attempted assault, leading to Joseph's **imprisonment** (Genesis 39:7-20). Egyptian punishments for slaves, including imprisonment or execution for such alleged offenses, are well documented. The account mentions Joseph being confined in the **prison house attached to the household of the chief of the guard**, likely a **state prison** where political prisoners and royal offenders were held.

This imprisonment was not random injustice but another step through which **Jehovah was preparing to elevate Joseph**, demonstrating that divine providence operates even in the darkest circumstances.

### Joseph's Administration: From Prison to Prime Minister

Joseph's God-given ability to interpret dreams—an ability that the **magicians and wise men of Egypt could not replicate**—brought him to Pharaoh's attention when Pharaoh was troubled by two prophetic dreams concerning the **seven years of abundance followed by seven years of famine** (Genesis 41:1-8).

When Joseph was summoned from prison, he clarified that **the interpretation belonged to God, not to himself:**

"I am not the one! God will speak concerning Pharaoh's welfare." (Genesis 41:16)

This testimony contrasts sharply with the **Egyptian magicians' reliance on occult knowledge and divination** (compare Genesis 41:8; Exodus 7:11-12). Joseph's interpretation and subsequent advice—to appoint an overseer to manage the years of plenty and prepare for the famine—displayed **administrative wisdom** that impressed Pharaoh and his court.

Pharaoh responded by placing Joseph over all Egypt:

"You will personally be over my house, and all my people will obey your orders. Only as to the throne will I be greater than you." (Genesis 41:40)

Joseph was given:

- **A signet ring**, symbolizing royal authority.
- **Fine linen garments**, typical of Egyptian nobility.
- **A gold necklace**, signifying status.
- **An Egyptian name, Zaphenath-paneah**, likely meaning "God speaks and lives" or "Revealer of secrets."
- **Marriage to Asenath**, daughter of **Potiphera, priest of On (Heliopolis)**, integrating him into Egypt's priestly elite (Genesis 41:42-45).

The marriage to a daughter of a priest aligns with **Egyptian social practices**, where high officials were often connected to the religious establishment. Yet Scripture maintains Joseph's identity as a worshiper of Jehovah, and neither Joseph nor the inspired text gives any credence to Egyptian idolatry.

### Egyptian Society Reflected in Joseph's Account

Joseph's rise during this period is consistent with **Middle Kingdom Egypt's administrative structure**, where a **vizier or prime minister** could hold significant authority, overseeing taxation, agriculture, and labor. The economic management described—collection of surplus grain, centralized storage, and controlled distribution—fits what is known of Egyptian state control over agriculture.

The Bible's mention of **storehouses in cities throughout Egypt** (Genesis 41:48-49) and the people selling their land to Pharaoh during the famine (Genesis 47:13-20) echoes administrative practices documented in Middle Kingdom inscriptions, including **state-run granaries and centralized resource distribution**.

Joseph's policy of exchanging grain for livestock and land during the famine, leading to Pharaoh's ownership of nearly all the land (except that of the priests), created an economic structure that centralized power under Pharaoh—a condition attested in historical sources.

**Theological Themes: Sovereignty, Providence, and Reconciliation**

The Joseph narrative repeatedly emphasizes that **Jehovah was the true architect** behind Joseph's rise and the preservation of Israel. When Joseph later revealed himself to his brothers, he declared:

"Now, do not be upset or angry with yourselves because you sold me here, for God sent me ahead of you for the preservation of life… It was not you who sent me here, but God." (Genesis 45:5, 8)

This affirmation of divine sovereignty highlights one of the Bible's clearest examples of how **Jehovah's purposes overrule human evil**, turning it to the fulfillment of His covenant promises.

The account culminates in **reconciliation and restoration**, as Joseph forgave his brothers, provided for his family, and ensured their survival during the famine. The entry of **Jacob (Israel)** into Egypt with his household (Genesis 46:1-27) marked the beginning of the fulfillment of Jehovah's prophecy to Abraham that his descendants would reside in a foreign land for generations.

**Preservation of Covenant Identity**

Despite Joseph's position in the heart of Egyptian power and culture, the text remains clear that **his faith was firmly rooted in Jehovah**, not in Egypt's gods. This is most evident in Joseph's final instructions before his death:

"God will surely give attention to you, and you must take my bones up out of this place." (Genesis 50:24-25)

This request to be buried in the Promised Land—fulfilled during the Exodus (Exodus 13:19; Joshua 24:32)—testifies to Joseph's enduring **trust in Jehovah's covenant promises** and his rejection of assimilation into Egyptian religious culture.

### Historical Authenticity and Cultural Harmony

The details of Joseph's life in Egypt—his enslavement, imprisonment, rise to power, administrative policies, and the structure of Egyptian governance—all align with **what is known archaeologically about the Middle Kingdom period**. While specific Pharaohs are not named, the biblical narrative accurately reflects **social, economic, and political conditions** of the time.

This historical consistency affirms the **reliability of the biblical record** and demonstrates that the events described are not mythological but deeply grounded in the historical realities of the ancient Near East.

Joseph's journey from **enslavement to exaltation in Egypt** is not merely an account of personal triumph but a profound demonstration of **Jehovah's sovereign hand at work in history**, preserving the line through which the covenant promises would be fulfilled. The narrative reveals Egypt's wealth, power, and administrative complexity, yet it simultaneously exposes the **spiritual emptiness of Egyptian religion** and the superiority of the worship of the true God.

Joseph's faithfulness, humility, and acknowledgment of divine providence stand as enduring examples for God's people, affirming that **Jehovah can work through any circumstance, even the wicked intentions of men, to accomplish His redemptive plan.**

# CHAPTER 14 What Is the Historical Significance of the Hyksos Period, and How Does It Relate to the Biblical Account of Joseph and Israel in Egypt?

**The Hyksos Period**

The historical period known as the **Hyksos Period** remains one of the most debated and least understood phases in Egyptian history. The Hyksos, whose name has been variously interpreted as "**Shepherd Kings**," "**Rulers of Foreign Lands**," or more precisely "**Rulers of the Uplands**," were foreign rulers of largely **Asiatic (Semitic) origin** who gained control over **northern Egypt**, particularly the **Nile Delta region**, during what is conventionally dated between the **Thirteenth and Seventeenth Dynasties**. Their rule is estimated to have lasted between **one to two centuries**, depending on scholarly interpretation.

The possibility that **Joseph's rise to power and Israel's early sojourn in Egypt** occurred during this period has often been suggested by commentators seeking to reconcile the biblical account with secular Egyptian history. However, this suggestion, while interesting, is fraught with uncertainty due to the **lack of reliable contemporary Egyptian records** and the speculative nature of the surviving historical sources. The biblical text itself does not specify the ethnic identity of the Pharaohs during Joseph's time, nor does it indicate any reliance on foreign rulers' favor to explain Joseph's appointment. Instead, Scripture attributes Joseph's rise to the **providence of Jehovah alone** (Genesis 45:7-9).

**Who Were the Hyksos?**

The name **Hyksos** derives from the Egyptian expression *Hik-khoswet*, meaning "**Rulers of Foreign Lands**." Egyptian documents from the **New Kingdom** period, after the Hyksos expulsion, refer to these rulers disparagingly as **"Asiatics,"** suggesting their **non-Egyptian, likely Semitic origins**. The Hyksos period followed the

**Twelfth Dynasty**, a time of significant power and prosperity in Egypt. The means by which the Hyksos rose to prominence remains debated, with theories ranging from:

- **Swift military conquest using chariot warfare**,
- To a **slow infiltration of Semitic nomads or traders**,
- Or even a **coup d'état taking control of an existing government weakened by internal strife**.

Modern archaeological and textual analysis leans away from the theory of a massive violent invasion and tends to favor the view of a **gradual takeover by groups of Semitic peoples** who were already present in Egypt, perhaps as traders, settlers, or mercenaries.

This more moderate theory harmonizes with evidence showing significant **Semitic presence in Egypt** before and during the period traditionally associated with Hyksos rule. Some of these groups, possibly related to Canaanite or Amorite populations, may have settled in the **eastern Nile Delta**, the same region where Israel would later dwell in the land of **Goshen**.

### The Problem of Historical Sources: Manetho and Josephus

Much of the traditional understanding of the Hyksos comes from the work of the **Egyptian historian Manetho**, who wrote in Greek during the **third century B.C.E.**, long after the events he described. Unfortunately, Manetho's original work has not survived. What is known of it comes through later quotations, particularly those cited by **Josephus** in his work **Against Apion**.

Manetho, as quoted by Josephus, presents the Hyksos as brutal foreign invaders who conquered Egypt without resistance, destroyed cities, desecrated temples, and ruled from their capital at **Avaris** in the Delta. After a prolonged war, according to this account, the Egyptians finally besieged them and allowed them to leave peacefully, whereupon they migrated to **Judea** and allegedly built **Jerusalem**.

Josephus, attempting to defend the biblical narrative against critics, identifies the Hyksos with the **Israelites**, accepting certain parts of Manetho's account but rejecting its negative portrayal of the Hyksos as aggressors. Josephus prefers the translation of Hyksos as "**captive shepherds**" rather than "king-shepherds."

However, modern scholars widely agree that **Manetho's account is unreliable**, highly propagandistic, and shaped by **Egyptian priestly hostility toward past foreign rulers**. There is no credible historical evidence linking the **Israelites directly with the Hyksos dynasty**. The Hyksos expulsion and the Israelite Exodus are distinct events separated by **chronological and cultural differences**.

As **C. E. DeVries** noted in *The International Standard Bible Encyclopedia*:

"In attempting to correlate secular history with the biblical data, some scholars have tried to equate the expulsion of the Hyksos from Egypt with the Israelite Exodus, but the chronology rules out this identification, and other factors as well make this hypothesis untenable."

The Hyksos' origins remain speculative, with suggestions ranging from **Canaanite, Amorite, Syrian-Palestinian, Arabian, or Hittite elements**, but the most consistent evidence points to **Semitic peoples from the Levant**, bearing names and cultural traits familiar in the biblical world.

**Theological Reflection: Divine Providence, Not Political Favoritism**

Some commentators have argued that **Joseph's favorable treatment in Egypt** might be explained by the Hyksos being friendly Semitic rulers who favored their fellow Asiatics. However, this view is both speculative and unnecessary. The **Scriptures themselves attribute Joseph's rise to the sovereign will of Jehovah**, not to ethnic favoritism or political opportunism:

"It was not you who sent me here, but God." (Genesis 45:8)

The narrative emphasizes that **Pharaoh's recognition of Joseph's God-given wisdom**, not racial kinship or Hyksos sympathy, was the decisive factor in Joseph's elevation to power (Genesis 41:38-40). Whether Pharaoh was of native Egyptian or foreign Hyksos descent is irrelevant to the theological point of the text.

# THE EGYPTIAN EMPIRE

The desire to identify Joseph's Pharaoh as Hyksos, therefore, reflects an **external attempt to explain divine providence through human circumstances**, a tendency the Bible itself resists. The focus remains on **Jehovah's guidance and blessing**, not on political alliances or racial connections.

### Egyptian National Memory and Historical Distortion

It is important to recognize that **Egyptian historical records were often controlled by the priesthood**, who sought to **defend the honor of the Egyptian gods and monarchy**. After the devastating humiliation brought upon Egypt by the **Ten Plagues**, the **death of the firstborn**, and the **destruction of the Egyptian military at the Red Sea**, Egyptian historians would have faced the challenge of **explaining away such catastrophic defeats**.

In this light, the Hyksos narrative, as preserved by Manetho, may represent **a distorted national memory of the Israelite presence and Exodus**, recast through Egyptian propaganda. It would be characteristic of ancient political history, especially priestly-dominated histories, to **invert the narrative**, portraying the true victims (Israelites) as oppressors (Hyksos) and the true oppressors (Egyptians) as victims of aggression.

History offers many examples of such distortion, where **conquered peoples are vilified and blamed for calamities** inflicted by their oppressors. If the Israelites, through Jehovah's miraculous deliverance, devastated Egypt's economy, religious system, and military might, the Egyptian scribes would have had every incentive to obscure or invert the facts.

This possibility harmonizes with the Bible's report of Egypt's devastation, the loss of its firstborn, and the humiliation of its gods (Exodus 12:12), none of which would have been willingly recorded in official annals. Instead, **propagandistic retellings like Manetho's may reflect an attempt to save face**, assigning guilt to foreign "shepherd kings" rather than acknowledging Israel's God as the true cause of Egypt's downfall.

### The Hyksos and the Exodus: Distinct Events

Attempts to equate the **Hyksos expulsion with the Israelite Exodus** are flawed for several reasons:

1. **Chronological discrepancy**: The generally accepted dates for the Hyksos expulsion do not align with the biblical dating of the **Exodus in 1446 B.C.E.**.
2. **Geographical and political differences**: The Hyksos were rulers of Egypt's north; the Israelites were enslaved laborers, not rulers.
3. **Cultural mismatch**: The Hyksos, though Semitic, were not Hebrews and showed no connection to Israelite religious identity or practice.
4. **Lack of biblical identification**: The Scriptures never refer to Pharaoh as Hyksos or as foreign; instead, the biblical portrayal consistently presents Pharaoh as the representative of Egypt proper.

The biblical account does not require any explanation based on the Hyksos hypothesis. The **divine orchestration of Joseph's rise and Israel's sojourn** stands independently of Egyptian dynastic history, driven by Jehovah's covenant purpose rather than by political accidents.

The **Hyksos period**, while significant in Egyptian history as a time of foreign rule, does not provide the key to understanding Joseph's rise or the Exodus. Attempts to equate the Hyksos with the Israelites reflect **speculative efforts to explain biblical events through secular history**, rather than allowing the inspired text to speak for itself.

The Bible's presentation of Joseph's story remains clear: **his success was by Jehovah's hand, not due to political favoritism or ethnic kinship**. Though Semitic rulers may have occupied Egypt's throne at some point, the essential factor was not race or politics but **divine providence and faithfulness to the promises made to Abraham**.

The distortions of Egyptian historians like Manetho may well represent an **inverted recollection of Israel's true history in Egypt**, an attempt to obscure the reality of Egypt's failure before the God of Israel. But the inspired Scriptures preserve the accurate record, affirming that **Jehovah alone directs the course of nations and delivers His people according to His righteous will.**

# CHAPTER 15 What Does the Bible Reveal About Israel's Slavery in Egypt?

**Israel's Slavery**

The enslavement of the Israelites in Egypt stands as one of the most defining episodes of Old Testament history, shaping Israel's national identity and theology. Referred to repeatedly in Scripture as **"the house of slaves"** and **"the iron furnace"** (Exodus 13:3; Deuteronomy 4:20; Jeremiah 11:4; Micah 6:4), Egypt became synonymous with oppression, hard labor, and injustice. Yet it also became the stage upon which Jehovah displayed His power, justice, and mercy through the miraculous deliverance of His people.

The details provided in the biblical narrative, particularly in **Exodus 1–12**, reveal not only the historical reality of Israel's bondage but also its spiritual significance. This period of oppression serves as the background for the great redemptive act of the Old Testament—the **Exodus**—which stands as the foundational demonstration of Jehovah's role as **Deliverer and Sovereign Judge**.

**The Rise of a New Pharaoh and the Onset of Oppression**

Following the death of **Joseph** and his brothers, the Israelites continued to dwell in the land of **Goshen**, experiencing **fruitfulness and rapid population growth**:

"The Israelites were fruitful and multiplied greatly. They became extremely numerous, so that the land was filled with them." (Exodus 1:7)

This multiplication fulfilled Jehovah's promise to **Abraham** that his descendants would become as numerous as the stars (Genesis 15:5). However, their increase provoked fear among the Egyptians, particularly under the reign of a new Pharaoh:

"Then a new king, who did not know Joseph, came to power over Egypt." (Exodus 1:8)

The identity of this Pharaoh remains unspecified in Scripture, and neither this oppressor nor the later Pharaoh of the Exodus is named. This omission is significant, as Egyptian history was often written under priestly oversight, with deliberate **omissions of national defeats and embarrassments**. The absence of direct Egyptian confirmation of these events is consistent with the **propagandistic nature of ancient royal records**, especially following catastrophic failures like the Exodus plagues and military defeat at the Red Sea.

While **Rameses II** of the **Nineteenth Dynasty** has often been suggested as the Pharaoh of oppression because of the mention of **Pithom and Raamses** (Exodus 1:11), scholars such as **Merrill Unger** have rightly cautioned against this assumption. Given **Rameses II's known practice of taking credit for earlier achievements**, these sites likely predated him and may have been **rebuilt or expanded** during his reign. The biblical use of the name "Raamses" probably reflects the **district name already in use from the time of Joseph** (Genesis 47:11).

The lack of a specific Pharaoh's name prevents false focus on Egyptian dynastic glory and keeps attention squarely on **Jehovah's actions** as the central force in history.

### Harsh Labor and Systematic Oppression

Fearing the growing strength of the Israelites, the Egyptian leadership initiated a systematic program of **forced labor and population control**:

"So they appointed taskmasters over them to oppress them with forced labor, and they built storage cities for Pharaoh, namely Pithom and Raamses." (Exodus 1:11)

The Israelites were subjected to **crushing burdens**, compelled to make **bricks** and engage in construction work under **harsh conditions** (Exodus 5:6-18). Egyptian records from various periods attest to **state-organized labor projects**, including brickmaking, often by prisoners or captives. Scenes on tomb walls and inscriptions corroborate the use of foreigners as conscripted laborers.

The intensification of oppression reflects not only Pharaoh's political strategy but also his attempt to **thwart Jehovah's blessing of Israelite multiplication**. However, Scripture notes that this effort backfired:

"But the more they oppressed them, the more they multiplied and spread." (Exodus 1:12)

This theme of **human opposition failing to frustrate divine purpose** recurs throughout biblical history, affirming Jehovah's sovereign control.

### Infanticide as State Policy

When forced labor failed to reduce Israel's population growth, Pharaoh resorted to **infanticide**—a genocidal policy targeting the male offspring of the Hebrews:

"Every newborn son that is born to the Hebrews you must throw into the Nile, but you may keep every daughter alive." (Exodus 1:22)

This cruel decree reflects the **utter moral bankruptcy of Egyptian leadership**. While Egyptian texts depict Pharaohs as divine protectors of Ma'at (order and justice), the biblical account exposes their hypocrisy and tyranny.

The act of casting male infants into the Nile may have had religious overtones, as the Nile was revered as a divine source of life and fertility. Pharaoh's decree, therefore, represented not only political expediency but also a form of **blasphemous corruption of Egyptian religious ideology**, turning the sacred river into an instrument of mass murder.

This policy sets the stage for **Moses' own birth and deliverance**, as his mother, in defiance of Pharaoh's order, placed him in a papyrus ark on the Nile (Exodus 2:3), symbolically casting her trust upon Jehovah for his preservation.

### Egyptian Silence and the Historical Record

The absence of Egyptian inscriptions acknowledging this oppression, the plagues, or the Exodus itself is consistent with Egyptian practice. Defeats were often **omitted, reinterpreted, or**

**erased** from official accounts. This is seen in other historical periods of Egyptian history, where military disasters were deliberately unrecorded or covered with triumphant inscriptions regardless of the actual outcome.

Egypt's **theological system**, rooted in the divine status of Pharaoh and the gods of Egypt, could not admit such humiliating failure without **undermining its religious legitimacy**. Thus, the biblical account stands as an honest witness, exposing the failures of Egyptian gods and Pharaoh's impotence before Jehovah.

### Connection to the Amarna Letters and the "Habiru"

The discovery of the **Amarna Tablets**, dating to the fourteenth century B.C.E. and found at **Tell el-Amarna**, has fueled speculation about potential connections between the **Habiru ('apiru)** mentioned in these texts and the Israelites. These tablets, primarily correspondence between **Canaanite rulers and Pharaoh Akhenaton**, describe raids and unrest involving groups called the Habiru.

However, careful examination of these texts shows that the **Habiru** were not an ethnic group but rather **bands of displaced peoples, raiders, or mercenaries** active across the Levant. Their activities do not match the **biblical conquest led by Israel** under Joshua, nor do they align with the sequence or theology of the biblical narrative. Attempts to equate the **Habiru with Hebrews (Israelites)** are speculative and not supported by the text itself.

Thus, while the Amarna Letters provide valuable background about the political instability of Canaan, they should not be conflated with the Israelite experience.

### The Lasting Impact of Israel's Oppression

Israel's oppression in Egypt became an enduring symbol of **human injustice and divine deliverance**. Jehovah's acts of judgment upon Egypt and His mighty hand of deliverance shaped Israel's collective memory and national identity:

"I am Jehovah your God, who brought you out of the land of Egypt, out of the house of slavery." (Exodus 20:2)

This reality was **memorialized annually in the Passover observance** (Exodus 12:1-27; Deuteronomy 16:1-3), which commemorated not only deliverance but also Jehovah's judgment against Egypt's gods (Exodus 12:12). The experience informed Israel's ethics, particularly in their treatment of **foreigners, slaves, and the poor** (Exodus 22:21; Leviticus 19:33-34; Deuteronomy 15:12-15).

The Exodus event, rooted in Israel's slavery, was repeatedly cited by prophets and psalmists as proof of Jehovah's power and faithfulness:

"He performed his signs among them... He struck down all the firstborn in their land, the firstfruits of all their vigor." (Psalm 78:43, 51)

"Give thanks to Jehovah, for he is good... To him who struck down Egypt's firstborn... and brought Israel out from their midst with a strong hand and an outstretched arm." (Psalm 136:1, 10-12)

This redemptive history became **theological grounding** for Israel's understanding of Jehovah as **Redeemer, Lawgiver, and Deliverer**, echoed even in later promises of restoration from exile (Jeremiah 16:14-15).

The **enslavement of Israel in Egypt**, though a dark chapter of suffering, stands as one of the most significant events in biblical history. It reveals the **oppressive nature of human power structures** when divorced from divine righteousness and contrasts human tyranny with the **steadfast love and justice of Jehovah**.

Egypt's failure to record this oppression, or the miraculous deliverance that followed, is no surprise given their historical methods of record-keeping and priestly control over public memory. Yet the biblical witness remains clear, consistent, and theologically profound: Jehovah alone is God, and **no human power, however great, can stand against His will**.

The Exodus from Egypt, born out of this oppression, remains the **paradigmatic act of divine salvation in the Hebrew Scriptures**, foreshadowing the ultimate deliverance that would be accomplished through the Messiah.

# CHAPTER 16 What Role Did Egypt Play After Israel's Conquest of Canaan?

### After Israel's Conquest of Canaan

Following the **Exodus from Egypt in 1446 B.C.E.** and the subsequent **forty years of wilderness wandering**, Israel, under the leadership of **Joshua**, began the conquest of **Canaan** around **1406 B.C.E.** This event marked the fulfillment of Jehovah's promise to give the land to Abraham's descendants (Genesis 12:7; Joshua 21:43-45). However, Israel's departure from Egypt and the conquest of Canaan did not entirely sever Egyptian involvement in the region. Egypt, though devastated by the plagues and the destruction of its military force at the Red Sea (Exodus 14:28), continued to pursue its political and military interests in **Canaan and surrounding territories** during the centuries that followed.

Egypt's activities after Israel's conquest reveal both **direct and indirect influence** over the Levant. These interactions are evidenced through biblical references, archaeological data, and Egyptian records. Understanding this period illuminates the **geopolitical backdrop** against which much of the **period of the Judges** and the early **monarchy of Israel** unfolded.

### Egyptian Influence in Canaanite Territories

Archaeological evidence and Egyptian inscriptions, particularly from the **Eighteenth Dynasty** and into the **Nineteenth Dynasty**, confirm that Egypt maintained control over various parts of **Canaan and southern Syria** through a network of **vassal city-states**, local rulers, and military garrisons. These city-states regularly corresponded with the Egyptian court, as seen in the **Amarna Tablets**, which date from the fourteenth century B.C.E., during the reign of **Pharaoh Akhenaton**.

These tablets, discovered at **Tell el-Amarna**, contain diplomatic letters from **Canaanite rulers** pleading for Egyptian assistance against raiders, including the **Habiru ('apiru)**. While some scholars once suggested the Habiru might be identified with the Hebrews, the biblical account of Israel's conquest does not align with the portrayal of the Habiru as **bands of mercenaries and raiders**, sometimes fighting alongside or against various Canaanite factions. The Habiru references appear across **a wide geographic region**, including areas far beyond Israel's sphere of operations, such as **Byblos in northern Lebanon**, making it unlikely that the term refers specifically to the Israelites.

Nevertheless, the Amarna correspondence reflects **political instability in Canaan** and Egypt's **ongoing, though weakening, control**. The weakening of Egyptian power during this time corresponds well with the opportunity Israel had to establish itself in the land without significant external military interference from Egypt.

### Egypt's Limited Response to Israel's Conquest

Strikingly, the biblical narrative records **no Egyptian military response** to Israel's conquest of Canaan. The absence of such intervention is noteworthy given Egypt's traditional interest in dominating the region. This silence may reflect the **internal weaknesses** Egypt faced at the time, including religious turmoil under Akhenaton and the political fragmentation that followed.

The Egyptian empire was preoccupied with **internal instability** and struggles with other external threats, particularly from **Hittite expansion into Syria**. These factors likely explain Egypt's failure to confront Israel militarily during the conquest period.

This situation aligns with Jehovah's providence, fulfilling His promise that **He would drive out the nations before Israel** (Deuteronomy 7:1-2) and that no foreign power would successfully stand against His people as they occupied the land (Joshua 23:9-10).

### Continuing Egyptian Presence in the Southern Levant

Although Egypt did not confront Israel directly during the initial conquest, evidence suggests that **Egyptian cultural and political influence** remained in certain regions of the Levant, particularly in the **southern coastal plain** and **along key trade routes**. Egyptian artifacts, scarabs, and inscriptions have been found at various sites in

## THE EGYPTIAN EMPIRE

**southern Canaan**, indicating Egypt's lingering presence or at least its economic interactions.

For example, archaeological discoveries at **Beth Shean**, located strategically near the Jordan Valley, reveal evidence of an **Egyptian administrative outpost** during this period. Such outposts helped Egypt maintain some measure of control over critical points of trade and military logistics.

However, this Egyptian foothold did not extend into the **central hill country of Canaan**, where Israel established its primary settlements. This geographical reality reinforces the biblical portrayal of Israel's dominance in these areas without significant Egyptian interference.

### Egypt During the Period of the Judges

Throughout the **period of the Judges**, which followed the conquest, Egypt did not play a central role in the oppression of Israel. Instead, Israel's struggles were primarily against regional powers such as the **Moabites, Midianites, Ammonites, and Philistines** (Judges 3–16). The absence of Egypt from these conflicts further suggests that **Egypt's imperial ambitions in Canaan had significantly diminished**.

Egypt's internal condition during this era, marked by dynastic decline and occasional resurgences, likely prevented any consistent military campaigns into Canaan. Only in later biblical history, particularly during the **united monarchy of Israel under Solomon**, does Egypt reemerge more clearly as a political player in Israel's affairs (1 Kings 3:1).

### Egypt's Later Encounters with Israel and Judah

Egypt's involvement with Israel intensified again during the **time of Solomon and Rehoboam**. Solomon's **marriage alliance with Pharaoh's daughter** (1 Kings 3:1) and the presence of Egyptian military campaigns in the days of **Shishak (Sheshonq I)** (1 Kings 14:25-26) reflect a return of Egypt to Levantine affairs. However, this development took place **centuries after the conquest period**.

Throughout the monarchy, Egypt fluctuated between periods of strength and weakness, at times acting as a buffer against **Assyrian or Babylonian aggression**, and at other times directly influencing the southern kingdom of Judah.

Yet the memory of Egypt as the place of Israel's enslavement remained central to Israel's theology, shaping their understanding of political entanglements with Egypt as dangerous compromises (Isaiah 30:1-5; 31:1-3; Ezekiel 17:15-18).

**Theological Significance: Egypt as the Archetype of Human Oppression**

In the prophetic literature and throughout the Psalms, Egypt continued to represent **oppressive human power that resists the rule of Jehovah**. The Exodus event became the pattern by which God's people were to understand deliverance, and Egypt symbolized not merely a geographic or political enemy but the embodiment of **worldly power in rebellion against God**.

This enduring symbol warns against alliances with Egypt, as seen in the later history of both Israel and Judah. The prophets condemned reliance on Egypt instead of trust in Jehovah (Isaiah 36:6; Hosea 7:11-16). This theological perspective reflects a consistent biblical message: **salvation does not come through political alliances or military might but through faithfulness to Jehovah**.

**Conclusion**

After Israel's conquest of Canaan, Egypt continued to exert **limited influence** in the region, particularly along the coast and through trade, but was **incapable of significant military intervention** during the early settlement period. The absence of Egyptian resistance to Israel's conquest aligns with both the **archaeological record** and the **theological claims of Scripture**—that Jehovah Himself granted the land to Israel, undeterred by the might of surrounding nations.

Egypt's role shifted from direct oppressor to a symbol of foreign entanglement and misplaced trust throughout Israel's subsequent history. Yet the memory of Israel's **enslavement and deliverance**

**from Egypt** remained central to their national identity and religious life, shaping their understanding of Jehovah's justice, power, and mercy.

The biblical account stands consistent with the historical evidence, affirming that the Exodus, conquest, and subsequent history unfolded not by human politics but by **the determined will of the Sovereign Creator**.

Edward D. Andrews

# CHAPTER 17 How Did Egypt Respond to the Assyrian Invasion and What Was Its Role in Israel's History During This Period?

**The Assyrian Invasion**

The period of **Assyrian dominance in the Near East**, particularly during the **eighth and seventh centuries B.C.E.**, profoundly shaped the political and military landscape of the ancient world. The rise of the **Neo-Assyrian Empire**, beginning with kings such as **Tiglath-Pileser III (745–727 B.C.E.)**, and extending through **Shalmaneser V (727–722 B.C.E.)**, **Sargon II (722–705 B.C.E.)**, **Sennacherib (705–681 B.C.E.)**, and **Esarhaddon (681–669 B.C.E.)**, brought devastating campaigns against **Israel, Judah, and neighboring regions**.

Egypt's involvement during this time reflects both its **ambition to reassert influence in the Levant** and its **repeated failure to provide effective support** to smaller states like Israel and Judah. Egypt's role during the **Assyrian invasions** serves as a sobering example of political maneuvering without spiritual foundation, consistent with the biblical warnings against trusting in Egypt rather than relying upon Jehovah.

**Assyria's Expansion and the Fall of Israel**

The Assyrian Empire's expansion into **Syria-Palestine** culminated in the destruction of the **northern kingdom of Israel** in **722 B.C.E.**, under the reign of **Shalmaneser V** and completed by **Sargon II**. The capital city, **Samaria**, fell after a prolonged siege, and the Israelite population was deported into various parts of the Assyrian Empire (2 Kings 17:5-6). The biblical account explicitly attributes Israel's downfall to **their apostasy and failure to remain faithful to Jehovah**:

# THE EGYPTIAN EMPIRE

"Jehovah warned Israel and Judah through all his prophets and every visionary, saying: 'Turn back from your wicked ways and keep my commandments, my statutes.' But they did not listen... So Jehovah removed Israel from his sight." (2 Kings 17:13-18)

During this critical period, Egypt offered **no effective assistance** to the northern kingdom. Although Egypt had long-standing interests in the Levant, including alliances with certain vassal states, its ability to counter Assyrian power was limited. Egypt's fragmented political situation during the **Twenty-Third and Twenty-Fourth Dynasties**, alongside internal struggles between **Libyan and Nubian rulers**, reduced its capacity for decisive military action.

### Egypt's Role During Judah's Crisis Under Sennacherib

Following the fall of Samaria, the Assyrians turned their attention to the **southern kingdom of Judah**, particularly during the reign of **Hezekiah** (c. 729–697 B.C.E.). Judah faced Assyrian aggression under **Sennacherib**, who invaded Judah and laid siege to **Jerusalem** in **701 B.C.E.** (2 Kings 18:13-17; Isaiah 36:1).

The Bible records that **Hezekiah initially sought to appease Sennacherib** by paying tribute (2 Kings 18:14-16). However, despite the tribute, the Assyrians continued their campaign, besieging fortified cities throughout Judah, including **Lachish**, famously depicted in Sennacherib's palace reliefs at **Nineveh**.

During this crisis, **Egyptian military forces** under **Tirhakah**, referred to as **"king of Cush"** (2 Kings 19:9; Isaiah 37:9), are mentioned as approaching to aid Judah. Tirhakah, though later king of Egypt and Cush, may have been functioning at this time as a **military commander or prince of the Cushite dynasty**. Egypt and Cush were politically united during the **Twenty-Fifth (Nubian) Dynasty**, a period when Nubian kings ruled from **Napata and Thebes** and sought to project influence into the Levant.

Despite Egypt's intervention, the **Assyrian military remained dominant**, and Sennacherib's forces continued their campaign. However, Jehovah decisively intervened:

"Then the angel of Jehovah went out and struck down 185,000 men in the camp of the Assyrians." (Isaiah 37:36)

Sennacherib withdrew to **Nineveh**, and Judah was spared—not by Egyptian aid, but by **Jehovah's power alone**. The account confirms the prophetic rebuke of **relying on Egypt**, as voiced by Isaiah:

"Woe to those who go down to Egypt for help, who rely on horses, who trust in chariots because they are many, and in horsemen because they are very mighty, but they do not look to the Holy One of Israel, nor seek Jehovah." (Isaiah 31:1)

Egypt's political ambitions, though present, were insufficient to challenge Assyria's supremacy. More importantly, Egypt's involvement is portrayed in Scripture as **unreliable and spiritually misguided**, reinforcing the principle that trust must be placed solely in Jehovah.

**Egypt's Diplomatic Engagements and the Failure of Alliances**

The period of Assyrian expansion was marked by **diplomatic maneuvering** as smaller states sought alliances to resist Assyrian power. Judah, at various times, looked toward Egypt for support, a policy sharply condemned by the prophets.

The **prophet Hosea**, writing earlier during the time of the northern kingdom's decline, warned:

"Ephraim has become like a silly dove without heart; they call to Egypt, they go to Assyria." (Hosea 7:11)

Similarly, **Isaiah** condemned Judah's diplomatic overtures to Egypt:

"Look! You trusted in the support of Egypt and the multitude of chariots, and in their horsemen, but they will all stumble." (Isaiah 30:1-7)

These prophetic denunciations reflect a consistent biblical theme: **deliverance does not come through human alliances but through obedience and reliance upon Jehovah alone.**

# THE EGYPTIAN EMPIRE

Egypt's political and military unreliability was not merely a political reality but a theological issue—Egypt symbolized **misplaced trust and false security**. Its failure to defend Judah in the face of Assyrian aggression validated the prophetic warnings.

### Assyria's Control Over Egypt and the Later Campaigns

During the reign of **Esarhaddon (681–669 B.C.E.)**, Assyria moved beyond controlling the Levant and launched military campaigns directly into **Egyptian territory**. Esarhaddon successfully invaded Egypt, capturing **Memphis** in **671 B.C.E.**, and installed **Assyrian vassals** in parts of Egypt. His son **Ashurbanipal (669–627 B.C.E.)** continued these campaigns, defeating **Tantamani**, the last ruler of the Twenty-Fifth Dynasty.

Assyrian inscriptions, including the **Annals of Esarhaddon**, detail these campaigns, highlighting Egypt's political instability and its failure to maintain independence. By this time, Egypt was effectively a **client state under Assyrian control**, with its internal rulers functioning under Assyrian oversight.

This historical reality further underscores the **futility of trusting Egypt for protection**, as warned repeatedly by Israelite prophets.

### Theological Reflection: Egypt's Role in the Shadow of Assyria

The Assyrian invasion period solidified Egypt's biblical portrayal as an **untrustworthy political ally and a spiritually corrupt nation**. Egypt's inability to provide effective resistance against Assyria demonstrated the emptiness of **political solutions apart from faith in Jehovah**.

The prophets' messages consistently returned to the lesson that **salvation belongs to Jehovah** and that **human alliances, military might, and diplomatic schemes** are powerless to secure deliverance apart from His will.

This theme is not merely historical but theological—underscoring that **Jehovah alone is King of the nations**, and **His purposes cannot be thwarted by earthly powers** (Isaiah 40:15-17).

The **Assyrian invasion** and Egypt's involvement during this period reveal the contrast between **earthly power struggles and divine sovereignty**. Egypt's repeated failure to protect Israel and Judah against Assyria confirmed the prophetic warnings against seeking security through human alliances. Though Egypt postured as a regional power, it was unable to stand before the might of Assyria or to provide meaningful assistance to Judah.

Jehovah's deliverance of Jerusalem during Sennacherib's siege stands as a monumental testimony that **salvation does not come through horses, chariots, or foreign kings but through the intervention of the living God**. Egypt's role serves as a historical illustration of the consequences of **placing trust in human power rather than divine promise**, a lesson continually echoed throughout the pages of Scripture.

# CHAPTER 18 How Did Egypt Suffer Defeat by Nebuchadnezzar, and What Was Its Role in the Fall of Judah?

### Egypt's Defeat by Nebuchadnezzar

The defeat of **Egypt** by **Nebuchadnezzar II**, king of **Babylon** (reigned 605–562 B.C.E.), marks a critical turning point in both **Egyptian and Israelite history**. Egypt, long portrayed in Scripture as a symbol of human power and false security, experienced humiliation and military defeat at the hands of Babylon, fulfilling **divinely inspired prophecy** and proving the futility of trusting in Egypt for political salvation.

The Babylonian Empire, under Nebuchadnezzar, emerged as the dominant power in the Near East following the collapse of the **Neo-Assyrian Empire**, filling the power vacuum that Assyria's fall had left. Egypt, weakened but still ambitious, sought to **reassert its influence over the Levant**, especially over Judah and the surrounding regions, but was ultimately unable to resist Babylon's advance.

The Bible clearly presents Egypt's downfall to Babylon as part of **Jehovah's sovereign judgment**, not only against Judah for its disobedience but also against Egypt itself for its arrogance, idolatry, and oppressive past.

### Egypt's Ambitions and the Battle of Carchemish

The background to Egypt's defeat by Babylon lies in the **Battle of Carchemish**, a decisive confrontation that took place in **605 B.C.E.** at Carchemish, a city located on the **Euphrates River**. Egypt, under **Pharaoh Necho II** (reigned 610–595 B.C.E.), had marched north to aid the remnants of the Assyrian forces, hoping to curb Babylonian expansion and maintain Egyptian influence over Syria-Palestine.

The historical record, including Babylonian chronicles, confirms that **Nebuchadnezzar led the Babylonian army to victory at**

**Carchemish**, decisively defeating Necho's forces and effectively ending Egypt's hopes of regaining dominance over the former Assyrian territories. This aligns perfectly with the biblical narrative, where the prophet **Jeremiah** foretold the humiliation of Egypt:

"Prepare buckler and shield, and advance for battle! Harness the horses; mount, O horsemen! Take your positions with helmets on, polish your spears, put on your armor! Why have I seen it? They are dismayed and have turned backward. Their mighty men are beaten down and have fled in haste; they look not back—terror on every side! declares Jehovah." (Jeremiah 46:3-5)

The **Battle of Carchemish** marked the end of Egypt's imperial ambitions in the Near East. From this point forward, Babylon became the uncontested dominant power, and Egypt was reduced to a **secondary regional player**, unable to protect its allies or vassal states.

### Egypt's Failure as Judah's False Hope

Despite Egypt's weakened state, Judah's kings, particularly **Jehoiakim**, **Jehoiachin**, and **Zedekiah**, continued to pursue political alliances with Egypt in the hope of resisting Babylonian domination. This policy was repeatedly condemned by the prophets as an act of **faithlessness toward Jehovah**, who had warned against relying on Egypt.

The prophet **Ezekiel** issued stern rebukes against Judah's reliance on Egypt:

"Then all the inhabitants of Egypt will know that I am Jehovah, because they have been a staff of reed to the house of Israel. When they grasped you by the hand, you broke and tore open their shoulders; and when they leaned on you, you broke and made all their hips unsteady." (Ezekiel 29:6-7)

Egypt is here portrayed as **unreliable and treacherous**, unable to provide the support that Judah expected. The **"staff of reed"** imagery emphasizes Egypt's fragility and impotence.

Jeremiah similarly denounced Judah's political dependence on Egypt, declaring:

# THE EGYPTIAN EMPIRE

"Woe to those who go down to Egypt for help, relying on horses, trusting in chariots because they are many and in horsemen because they are very strong, but who do not look to the Holy One of Israel or seek Jehovah!" (Isaiah 31:1; compare Jeremiah 2:18, 36-37)

These prophetic warnings make it clear that **Egypt's defeat was not only military but also theological**—a demonstration that trust in human power rather than Jehovah leads to disaster.

**Babylon's Invasion of Egypt and Fulfillment of Prophecy**

Nebuchadnezzar's defeat of Egypt was not limited to the Battle of Carchemish. Subsequent Babylonian campaigns continued to press into Egyptian territory. The book of **Jeremiah** records Jehovah's declaration of Egypt's coming judgment:

"Declare in Egypt, and proclaim in Migdol, proclaim in Memphis and Tahpanhes; say, 'Take your stand and be ready, for the sword shall devour all around you.'" (Jeremiah 46:14)

Further, Jehovah announced through Jeremiah that **Nebuchadnezzar would invade Egypt** and bring devastation:

"Nebuchadnezzar king of Babylon will come against Egypt with great power, with chariots and horsemen and with a great multitude. He will kill with the sword those appointed for slaughter… I will set fire to the temples of the gods of Egypt, and he shall burn them and carry them away captive." (Jeremiah 43:10-13)

Although Egyptian sources remain silent regarding these humiliations—consistent with their pattern of avoiding records of military defeat—Babylonian inscriptions support the reality of Nebuchadnezzar's campaigns reaching **Egyptian territory**.

The Babylonian Chronicles report that after Nebuchadnezzar secured his dominance over **Judah**, including the **destruction of Jerusalem in 587 B.C.E.**, he pursued military action against Egypt as a continuation of his strategy to control the Levant fully.

The historical fulfillment of these prophecies, even in the absence of detailed Egyptian accounts, confirms the **accuracy of the biblical record** and the authority of Jehovah's Word.

**Egypt's Ongoing Weakness and Jehovah's Pronouncement**

The prophet **Ezekiel**, writing during the Babylonian exile, delivered an extended oracle against Egypt (Ezekiel 29–32). Jehovah likened Egypt to a **great monster lying in the midst of its rivers**, boasting of its self-sufficiency:

"Behold, I am against you, Pharaoh king of Egypt, the great dragon that lies in the midst of his streams, that says, 'My Nile is my own; I made it for myself.'" (Ezekiel 29:3)

Ezekiel foretold that Egypt would be **desolate for forty years**, scattered among the nations, and reduced to a lowly kingdom:

"I will scatter the Egyptians among the nations and disperse them throughout the countries… It shall be the lowliest of the kingdoms, and it shall never again exalt itself above the nations." (Ezekiel 29:12, 15)

This prophecy aligns with Egypt's subsequent history. Although Egypt remained an inhabited land, it never regained its former imperial stature. Under the **Babylonians**, and later under the **Persians**, **Greeks**, and **Romans**, Egypt became increasingly subject to foreign rule, fulfilling the scriptural declaration that it would never again rise as a dominant power.

**Egypt and the Remnant of Judah**

One of the final episodes linking Egypt to the fall of Judah was the **flight of Jewish refugees into Egypt after the destruction of Jerusalem**. Against Jehovah's explicit command, survivors, including **Jeremiah**, were taken by force or fled into Egypt seeking refuge (Jeremiah 42–43).

Jehovah's judgment followed them there:

"If you set your faces to enter Egypt and go to live there, then the sword that you fear shall overtake you there in the land of Egypt, and the famine of which you are afraid shall follow close after you to Egypt, and there you shall die." (Jeremiah 42:15-16)

The remnant's rebellion against Jehovah's word and their false hope in Egypt's protection only brought further disaster,

# THE EGYPTIAN EMPIRE

demonstrating again that **Egypt could not shield them from divine judgment**.

Egypt's defeat by **Nebuchadnezzar** and its inability to protect Judah underscore one of the Bible's most consistent themes: **trust in human power, especially in pagan nations like Egypt, is folly**. Egypt's military ambitions, chariots, and horses proved useless against the determined judgment of Jehovah executed through Babylon.

The historical events confirm the **accuracy of prophetic warnings** issued by **Jeremiah, Ezekiel, and Isaiah**, demonstrating that political alliances, no matter how promising they appear, are worthless when opposed to God's declared will.

Egypt's failure to rise again as a dominant empire, its defeat at the hands of Nebuchadnezzar, and its repeated portrayal as unreliable in Scripture all affirm the truth that **Jehovah alone is Savior and Deliverer**, and those who seek refuge in human strength rather than divine promise will meet only ruin.

# CHAPTER 19 What Was Egypt's Role and Condition Under Persian Domination, and How Does This Fulfill Biblical Prophecy?

### Egypt Under Persian Domination

The subjugation of **Egypt under Persian rule** represents the final stage in the long historical trajectory of Egypt as a once-dominant power that, in fulfillment of biblical prophecy, was permanently humbled and reduced to a **secondary status among the nations**. This decline did not occur through random geopolitical shifts but through the **providential outworking of Jehovah's judgments**, repeatedly announced by His prophets, particularly **Jeremiah** and **Ezekiel**.

The rise of the **Persian Empire** under **Cyrus the Great (559–530 B.C.E.)**, followed by **Cambyses II (530–522 B.C.E.)** and later **Darius I (522–486 B.C.E.)**, brought Egypt fully under foreign domination. This fulfilled Jehovah's declaration that Egypt would be **"the lowliest of the kingdoms"** and that it would **never again dominate other nations** (Ezekiel 29:15). Egypt's history under the Persians affirms the truth of these prophetic pronouncements and serves as a continued demonstration of **God's control over the nations**.

### The Persian Conquest of Egypt

Following the collapse of the **Neo-Babylonian Empire** and the rise of Persia, the Persians quickly absorbed the former Babylonian territories, including dominion over **Judah and Jerusalem** after **Cyrus's decree** allowed the Jewish exiles to return in **537 B.C.E.** (Ezra 1:1-4). Egypt, however, remained outside Persian control until the reign of **Cambyses II**, the son of Cyrus.

In **525 B.C.E.**, Cambyses II launched a successful military campaign against **Egypt's Twenty-Sixth Dynasty**, ruled at that time by **Pharaoh Psamtik III**. The decisive **Battle of Pelusium** opened the gateway for Persian entry into Egypt. The Persian forces advanced with superior strategy and manpower, and Psamtik III was defeated, captured, and later executed.

Persian records, including the **Behistun Inscription** and Herodotus' account (though colored by Greek bias), confirm that Egypt was then incorporated into the **Achaemenid Empire** as one of its satrapies (provinces). Cambyses assumed the formal title of **"Pharaoh of Egypt"**, a political move aimed at legitimizing his rule among the Egyptian elite.

### Fulfillment of Ezekiel's Prophecy

The subjugation of Egypt under Persia stands as a **direct fulfillment of Ezekiel's prophecy**:

"It will become the lowliest of the kingdoms, and it will never again exalt itself above the nations; I will make them so small that they will not rule over the nations." (Ezekiel 29:15)

Despite its long history of imperial ambition and regional dominance, Egypt was reduced to a **subservient status under foreign rulers**. While Egypt remained inhabited and its cultural traditions continued, its **political independence was shattered**, and it never again rose to the imperial heights of its earlier dynasties.

The Egyptian priesthood, which had long intertwined its religious authority with political power, was now subordinated to Persian imperial administration. Local governance continued, but always under the oversight of Persian-appointed officials.

### Persian Control and Administrative Policies

The Persians governed Egypt with the same satrapal system they applied throughout their empire. Egypt became the **sixth satrapy**, and Persian rulers allowed a measure of local administration under strict Persian supervision. Egyptian religion was generally tolerated, but the **political and military power of Egypt remained firmly in Persian hands**.

During the rule of **Darius I**, inscriptions confirm Persian building projects in Egypt, including restorations of temples, which were intended to curry favor with the local population. However, despite these gestures, Egypt remained restive under foreign rule, and there were several **revolts against Persian authority**, though none succeeded in reestablishing Egypt as an independent power for any sustained period.

These failed revolts, such as those under **Petubastis III** and later during the reign of **Darius II**, demonstrated Egypt's inability to break free from the grip of Persian control. Each insurrection ended with Persian military intervention and the reassertion of imperial dominance.

The religious autonomy allowed by the Persians, including temple restorations, could not compensate for the **loss of national sovereignty**, nor could it alter the reality that Egypt's days of dominance were permanently over, just as Jehovah had declared.

**Egypt's Position Relative to Israel During Persian Rule**

While Egypt's political status diminished under Persia, **Judah's exiles were returning to their homeland** under Persian sanction, beginning with Cyrus's decree. Egypt, once the oppressor of Israel, now saw the **rebuilding of the temple in Jerusalem** (Ezra 6:3-5) and the restoration of worship to Jehovah proceed under the authority of a foreign empire that Egypt could not challenge.

This historical irony magnifies the **righteousness of Jehovah's judgments**. Egypt, which had enslaved Israel centuries earlier and had repeatedly been sought by Israelite kings as a false refuge, now stood **powerless to prevent the fulfillment of Jehovah's promises** regarding the restoration of His people.

Thus, the biblical theme remains consistent: salvation and restoration come **not through human alliances or earthly power, but solely by Jehovah's providence**.

**Continued Prophetic Condemnation of Egypt**

The humbled state of Egypt under Persia was not merely a political condition but a **manifestation of divine judgment**. The prophets, particularly **Jeremiah** and **Ezekiel**, repeatedly warned against reliance on Egypt, and history confirmed their warnings.

Egypt's inability to rise again as a superpower, even under periods of attempted resistance against Persian rule, validated the Word of Jehovah. Egypt's pride in its gods, its military strength, and its Nile-based economy proved useless in the face of **God's decrees against idolatry and arrogance.**

The imagery of Egypt as a **broken reed** (Isaiah 36:6) and a **great dragon pulled from its rivers and cast into the desert** (Ezekiel 29:3-5) became a lasting symbol of the **emptiness of human pride against divine authority.**

**Egypt's Further Subjugation and the End of Its Independence**

Though Egypt would briefly reassert local dynastic rule between **404 and 343 B.C.E.**, this period of autonomy was unstable and ended when **Persia reconquered Egypt under Artaxerxes III**. The reconquest confirmed that Egypt could not escape the cycle of **foreign domination** decreed by Jehovah.

Ultimately, Egypt fell under the control of **Alexander the Great** in **332 B.C.E.**, after the Persian Empire was defeated by the Macedonian forces. From that time onward, Egypt passed successively under the control of the **Ptolemies**, **Romans**, **Byzantines**, **Arabs**, and other foreign powers—all confirming Ezekiel's pronouncement that Egypt would never again rule the nations.

**Theological Significance of Egypt's Subjugation**

The subjugation of Egypt under Persia and later empires serves as a **powerful theological testimony** to the sovereignty of Jehovah over the nations. Egypt's decline was not merely geopolitical; it was a divine response to **centuries of pride, idolatry, oppression, and resistance to God's will**.

The biblical prophets consistently present Egypt as **a symbol of the futility of trusting in human strength**. Israel's history demonstrates that reliance on Egypt, instead of on Jehovah, led only to further ruin. Egypt's final status under Persian rule and beyond validated the **accuracy of biblical prophecy** and highlighted the unchanging truth that **Jehovah alone determines the rise and fall of nations** (Daniel 2:21).

Egypt's experience under Persian domination completed the prophetic picture of its **permanent humbling before Jehovah**. From the plagues of Moses' day to the defeats under Nebuchadnezzar and finally to the loss of independence under Persia, Egypt's history confirms the **infallibility of divine prophecy** and the certainty of God's justice.

Despite its ancient grandeur and cultural achievements, Egypt could not escape the consequences of its pride and opposition to Jehovah's will. Its failure to recover imperial dominance stands as a perpetual reminder that **the Most High is ruler in the kingdom of mankind and gives it to whomever He wills** (Daniel 4:17).

Egypt's story under Persian control, therefore, is not only a chapter of political history but a demonstration of **the hand of God in the affairs of nations**, teaching all who read the Scriptures that **deliverance and dominion belong to Jehovah alone**.

THE EGYPTIAN EMPIRE

# CHAPTER 20 What Was Egypt's Role and Condition Under Greek Rule, and How Did This Fulfill Biblical Patterns of Judgment?

**Egypt Under Greek Rule**

The conquest of Egypt by **Alexander the Great** in **332 B.C.E.** ushered in a new phase of Egyptian history, one that continued to validate the **biblical judgment pronounced by Jehovah** against the land of Egypt for its historic pride, idolatry, and persistent opposition to His will. Although Egypt remained culturally significant under **Greek rule**, politically it continued to experience the prophesied status of being **"the lowliest of the kingdoms"** (Ezekiel 29:15), never regaining its previous dominance over other nations.

Egypt's incorporation into the **Hellenistic world** was not an accident of political fortune but part of the broader outworking of Jehovah's sovereign control over the nations, as He "changes times and seasons, removes kings and sets up kings" (Daniel 2:21). Greek domination, which began with the arrival of **Alexander of Macedon**, represents yet another chapter in Egypt's long history of **foreign subjugation**, confirming the prophetic Word.

**Alexander's Conquest and the Founding of Alexandria**

After his victorious campaigns across the Persian Empire, **Alexander the Great** entered Egypt in **332 B.C.E.** to find little resistance. Egypt's Persian overlords had been widely resented, and Alexander was welcomed by the Egyptian priesthood, who saw in him an opportunity to restore some measure of local religious freedom, though under foreign control.

Alexander founded the city of **Alexandria** near the western edge of the Nile Delta, which became the principal city of Egypt under Greek rule. Designed as a **center of Greek administration,**

**commerce, and culture**, Alexandria quickly rose in prominence, overshadowing older Egyptian capitals like **Memphis** and **Thebes**.

Though Alexander's reign in Egypt was brief—he died in **323 B.C.E.** at the young age of 32—his conquest laid the groundwork for the **Ptolemaic Dynasty**, the Macedonian Greek line that would rule Egypt for the next three centuries.

### The Ptolemaic Dynasty: Foreign Rule Continued

Following Alexander's death, his empire was divided among his generals, with **Ptolemy I Soter** taking control of Egypt. The **Ptolemies**, though Greek in culture and language, adopted certain Egyptian religious titles and iconography to legitimize their rule. Nevertheless, Egypt remained firmly under **foreign domination**, consistent with Jehovah's decree that Egypt would never again exalt itself among the nations.

The Ptolemaic rulers ruled Egypt as **Hellenistic monarchs**, with a centralized administration based in Alexandria. Although the Ptolemies allowed the continuation of Egyptian religious practices and supported the temple complexes at places like **Philae and Karnak**, they ensured that **Greek culture and language dominated the political and intellectual life** of the country.

This period saw the construction of the famed **Library of Alexandria**, an institution that amassed a vast collection of texts, including many works translated into **Greek**, among them the **Septuagint (LXX)**—the Greek translation of the Hebrew Scriptures. This translation, produced in the **third to second centuries B.C.E.**, under the early Ptolemies, played a crucial role in making the Hebrew Scriptures accessible throughout the Greek-speaking world.

### Theological Reflection: Human Wisdom Versus Divine Revelation

The Ptolemaic period in Egypt was characterized by **intellectual flourishing**, with Alexandria becoming one of the major centers of **Greek philosophy, science, and learning**. Yet, from the biblical perspective, this human wisdom was powerless to challenge the **truth of divine revelation**.

# THE EGYPTIAN EMPIRE

The Apostle Paul, writing in the first century C.E., would later contrast the **world's wisdom** with the message of the cross:

"Where is the wise man? Where is the scribe? Where is the debater of this age? Has not God made foolish the wisdom of the world?" (1 Corinthians 1:20)

The Library of Alexandria and the intellectual endeavors of the Hellenistic world, while significant in secular terms, could not replace or rival the inspired truth of the Hebrew Scriptures. Egypt's supposed rebirth under Greek culture was merely another form of **external adornment without spiritual substance**, demonstrating again that **true wisdom begins with the fear of Jehovah** (Proverbs 1:7).

### Egypt and the Jewish Community During Ptolemaic Rule

During the Ptolemaic period, a significant **Jewish population resided in Egypt**, particularly in Alexandria. This community, descendants of earlier migrations and voluntary settlers, contributed to the cultural life of the city while retaining their religious identity. The production of the **Septuagint** reflects the reality that many Jews living in Egypt had adopted Greek as their primary language.

However, the presence of Jews in Egypt during this time does not suggest divine favor upon Egypt itself. Rather, it shows **Jehovah's providence in preserving His Word** even in the midst of foreign lands and among the dispersed Jewish people (compare Isaiah 11:11-12).

It is significant that the Jewish community in Egypt did not adopt Egyptian idolatry wholesale, a sharp contrast to Israel's earlier corruption while dwelling in Egypt before the Exodus (Ezekiel 20:7-8). Instead, many Jews in Alexandria maintained a connection to **Jerusalem and the temple worship** (though Hellenization pressures did lead to some compromises for certain individuals).

### Egypt's Continued Powerlessness and Internal Strife

Despite periods of relative stability under the early Ptolemies, the dynasty was plagued by **internal conflict, succession crises, and civil wars**. By the time of the later Ptolemies, including the notorious reign of **Cleopatra VII**, Egypt had become a pawn in the power struggles between **Rome and rival Hellenistic states**.

Egypt's failure to maintain stable rule or assert independence mirrors the biblical prophecy that Egypt would remain **a lowly kingdom, never again ruling over the nations** (Ezekiel 29:15). The political fragmentation and repeated dependence on foreign powers further confirmed the truth of Jehovah's Word.

**The Last Ptolemies and the End of Greek Rule**

The final stages of Greek rule in Egypt culminated in the reign of **Cleopatra VII** (51–30 B.C.E.). Her political maneuvering, including alliances with **Julius Caesar** and later **Mark Antony**, was an attempt to maintain Egypt's autonomy against the rising power of **Rome**.

However, following the **defeat of Antony and Cleopatra at the Battle of Actium in 31 B.C.E.**, Egypt was fully annexed into the **Roman Empire** by **Octavian (Augustus Caesar)** in **30 B.C.E.**, ending the Ptolemaic line. Egypt became a **Roman province**, governed directly by imperial officials.

Thus, even the last flicker of Egypt's political independence was extinguished, perfectly aligning with the long-standing prophetic declaration that Egypt would never again rise to imperial dominance.

Egypt's experience under Greek rule continues the **biblical testimony of Jehovah's judgment against the nations**. Despite the cultural grandeur of the **Hellenistic period**, Egypt remained politically subjugated, unable to restore its ancient imperial power. Its temporary moments of prestige under the Ptolemies could not reverse the divine sentence that Egypt would be **humbled among the nations**.

The intellectual accomplishments of Alexandria, including the Septuagint translation of the Hebrew Scriptures, served Jehovah's purpose in **spreading His Word throughout the Mediterranean world**, yet Egypt itself remained under judgment, unable to thwart the sovereign will of the true God.

The end of Greek rule and Egypt's absorption into the Roman Empire completed yet another stage of Egypt's historical trajectory as

**a nation brought low by divine decree**. This reality stands as an enduring reminder that **Jehovah governs the affairs of men** and that trust placed in human power, whether in Pharaohs, Greeks, or Romans, remains futile.

Egypt's story under Greek rule confirms the consistent message of Scripture: **"The nations are like a drop from a bucket, and are accounted as the dust on the scales"** (Isaiah 40:15). Only Jehovah's counsel stands forever (Psalm 33:10-11).

Edward D. Andrews

# CHAPTER 21 What Was Egypt's Condition Under Roman Rule, and How Did This Complete the Biblical Pattern of Judgment?

### Egypt Under Roman Rule

The annexation of Egypt by **Rome in 30 B.C.E.**, following the defeat of **Cleopatra VII** and **Mark Antony** at the **Battle of Actium**, marked the final stage of Egypt's long descent from imperial power to subjugated status—a descent foreseen by Jehovah through His prophets. Egypt, once the great empire of the ancient world, was reduced under Roman dominion to what Ezekiel had prophesied centuries earlier: **"the lowliest of the kingdoms"** (Ezekiel 29:15).

This period of **Roman rule**, while bringing a measure of administrative stability, continued the pattern of **foreign domination** that had characterized Egypt since the time of the Babylonians, Persians, and Greeks. Egypt's continued inability to rise again as an independent empire affirms the **faithfulness and reliability of biblical prophecy**, demonstrating that no human power could reverse the decree of Jehovah.

### Egypt Becomes a Roman Province

Following the deaths of **Cleopatra VII** and **Mark Antony**, **Octavian (later Augustus Caesar)** declared Egypt to be a **personal possession of the emperor**, not merely a typical senatorial province. This special status reflected both Egypt's strategic importance as the **breadbasket of the Roman Empire**—providing crucial grain supplies to Rome—and the historical precedent of Egypt as a land of centralized power.

Roman emperors strictly controlled access to Egypt, forbidding senators and equestrians to enter the province without imperial permission. A Roman **prefect (praefectus Aegypti)**, typically of equestrian rank, governed Egypt rather than a senatorial proconsul.

# THE EGYPTIAN EMPIRE

This structure ensured that Egypt remained tightly under the emperor's direct oversight, preventing the rise of potential rivals who might leverage Egypt's resources for rebellion.

The first prefect of Egypt was **Gaius Cornelius Gallus**, appointed by Augustus, and his successors maintained Roman order while respecting certain aspects of traditional Egyptian administration, particularly concerning taxation and temple economy.

## The Continuation of Religious Practices Under Roman Oversight

While the Roman emperors largely tolerated **Egyptian religious traditions**, including the worship of **Isis, Osiris, and Horus**, they did so within the strict limits of Roman control. Temples continued to function, and religious festivals were permitted, but there was no restoration of **Egyptian political autonomy or priestly power** in the governing structure.

Egypt's religion, even under Roman tolerance, remained **spiritually barren and morally corrupt**, echoing the earlier prophetic condemnations. The idolatrous system persisted, with animal worship, temple prostitution, and magic still entrenched, but devoid of any real influence upon Egypt's political standing.

Rome's pragmatic approach to religion did not reflect divine approval but merely political calculation. From a biblical perspective, Egypt's ongoing subjugation was evidence that its **idolatry and pride remained judged by Jehovah**, who alone holds power over the destiny of nations.

### Jewish Presence and Conflict in Roman Egypt

A significant **Jewish community** remained in Egypt during Roman rule, particularly concentrated in **Alexandria**. This community, which had existed since the **Ptolemaic period**, was initially permitted to flourish under Roman protection. However, tensions between the Jewish population and the **Greek Alexandrians** escalated under Roman administration.

Historical records, including those of **Philo of Alexandria**, a Jewish philosopher writing in the early first century C.E., describe these social and political frictions. The situation deteriorated significantly during the reign of **Caligula (37–41 C.E.)**, who ordered that his statue be placed in the temple at **Jerusalem** (an order never fulfilled due to his assassination). The anti-Jewish riots in Alexandria during this period reflected the broader instability of Egypt's multicultural society under Rome.

These Jewish-Greek tensions culminated in violent outbreaks during the **First Jewish War (66–73 C.E.)**, with riots spreading even into Egypt. Later revolts, such as the **Kitos War (115–117 C.E.)** during the reign of **Trajan**, saw further bloody conflicts between Jewish communities and the Roman authorities throughout the Diaspora, including Egypt.

Despite this continued Jewish presence, **Egypt itself never played a leading role in Jewish religious life**, as the temple in Jerusalem remained the true center of worship until its destruction in 70 C.E. Egypt's significance in this period remained secondary—a reminder that its former days of imperial strength had long passed.

**Egypt in New Testament Times**

Egypt features briefly but importantly in the **New Testament**, particularly in the **Gospel of Matthew**, where **Joseph, Mary, and the infant Jesus fled to Egypt** to escape the murderous plot of **Herod the Great** (Matthew 2:13-15). This event fulfilled the prophecy:

"Out of Egypt I called my son." (Hosea 11:1; quoted in Matthew 2:15)

This reference underscores Egypt's continuing symbolic role in biblical theology—as a place of **exile and oppression**, but also of **temporary refuge**, only to be left behind when Jehovah calls His people back to their proper place.

Egypt in the New Testament era, though under Roman control, retained its ancient character as **a land defined not by faithfulness to Jehovah but by idolatry, superstition, and political subjugation**.

Notably, the **Apostle Paul**, while traveling through various Roman provinces, did not emphasize Egypt as a center for Christian evangelism, focusing instead on the heart of the empire and major urban centers across Asia Minor, Greece, and Rome itself. This absence reflects the **theological marginalization of Egypt** in the redemptive history of the New Testament.

### The Final Collapse of Egyptian Identity Under Rome

By the later centuries of Roman rule, Egypt's unique identity as a distinct imperial power had fully dissolved. Though still culturally rich and economically valuable, Egypt had become fully absorbed into the Roman system. Its administrative function was purely provincial, with no capacity for independent political initiative.

The Roman emperors exploited Egypt's resources, especially grain, but imposed harsh taxation and strict military control. Egyptian rebellions against Rome were swiftly and brutally suppressed, and no serious effort at independence succeeded.

The **gradual spread of Christianity into Egypt** during the second and third centuries C.E. did not alter Egypt's political impotence but did introduce a new religious dynamic. Yet even the Christianization of Egypt in later centuries could not undo the prophetic judgment that the nation would **never again rule over the nations**.

### Theological Reflection: Egypt as a Permanent Example of Humbled Power

Egypt's history under Roman rule provides the final confirmation of the **biblical pattern of judgment** against a nation that exalted itself against Jehovah. Despite its vast contributions to art, science, and architecture, Egypt's political history stands as a testimony that **those who oppose the will of the true God cannot stand**.

The fate of Egypt echoes the broader principle expressed by **Daniel**:

"He changes times and seasons; he removes kings and sets up kings; he gives wisdom to the wise and knowledge to those who have understanding." (Daniel 2:21)

The Roman subjugation of Egypt—following the Babylonians, Persians, and Greeks—testifies to the futility of human pride, military might, and pagan religion when set against the sovereign decrees of the Creator. Egypt's golden age of the Pharaohs remained a distant memory, unable to return because of the enduring truth of **Jehovah's prophetic word**.

Even as Roman power itself would later fade, the biblical judgment upon Egypt remained evident: Egypt would never again dominate, never again wield imperial authority, and never again stand as a beacon of political or spiritual leadership among nations.

Egypt's subordination under Roman rule completes the arc of its long fall from ancient grandeur to enduring humiliation. This outcome was not merely historical but **theological**, demonstrating the righteousness of Jehovah's judgments and His sovereign authority over all kings and empires.

The prophetic declarations of **Ezekiel, Jeremiah, and Isaiah** found their final historical vindication in Egypt's continued decline under Rome. Egypt serves as a lasting illustration of the truth that **all nations are subject to the will of God**, and that no earthly power can overturn His decrees.

Thus, Egypt under Roman rule stands as the final historical chapter in the biblical portrayal of Egypt: once mighty, now lowly—a perpetual sign that **Jehovah alone is Sovereign**, and those who oppose Him will be brought down.

THE EGYPTIAN EMPIRE

# CHAPTER 22 What Do the Valuable Papyrus Finds Reveal About Egypt's History and the Reliability of the Biblical Record?

**Valuable Papyrus Finds**

The discovery of **papyrus documents** in Egypt over the last two centuries has provided a remarkable window into the life, administration, economy, religion, and social customs of the ancient Egyptians, as well as their interactions with surrounding peoples—including the Israelites. These finds, often preserved in the dry climate of Egypt's desert regions, stand as silent witnesses to a culture that, while materially sophisticated, remained spiritually blind in its opposition to Jehovah. In the providence of God, many of these documents corroborate elements of the **historical and cultural context** reflected in the Bible, demonstrating again that Scripture's portrayal of Egypt is reliable, grounded in reality, and free from the mythological distortions common to human traditions.

Papyrus, made from the **Cyperus papyrus plant** that thrived in the marshy regions of the **Nile Delta**, became Egypt's primary writing material as early as the third millennium B.C.E. This plant-based medium was cut into strips, pressed together, and dried to create sheets for writing. The ancient Hebrew term for the Nile plant, *gome'* (גֹּמֶא), appears in Exodus 2:3, where it is used to describe the basket in which **Moses** was placed by his mother—demonstrating the familiarity of the biblical writers with Egyptian materials and customs.

These papyrus documents, whether administrative, legal, literary, or religious, are not merely archaeological curiosities but important evidences that help illuminate the **background of biblical events**, the **political landscape of Egypt**, and the **practices of its people**.

**The Ebers Papyrus: Medical Superstition and Disease**

One of the most famous of the medical papyri is the **Ebers Papyrus**, dating to approximately the **sixteenth century B.C.E.** This document contains hundreds of medical prescriptions, including treatments for various diseases and injuries. While it demonstrates some empirical knowledge of medicinal herbs, it also reveals the **gross superstition and magical thinking** that characterized Egyptian medicine.

The Ebers Papyrus prescribes such remedies as applying **animal dung, crocodile excrement, and blood of various creatures** as treatments for ailments—practices that reflect the fundamental misunderstanding of health and disease in Egyptian thought. Incantations and spells are often prescribed alongside these treatments, illustrating the **prominent role of magic** in Egyptian healing practices.

The content of the Ebers Papyrus validates the biblical description of Egypt as a land of **"charmers" and "professional foretellers of events"** (Isaiah 19:3), steeped in occult practices rather than true understanding. In stark contrast, the **Mosaic Law** given to Israel prohibited such superstitions and presented far more advanced health regulations, such as sanitary quarantines (Leviticus 13–15) and dietary laws, showing the superiority of divine wisdom over human superstition.

### The Edwin Smith Surgical Papyrus: Practical Surgery and Misconceptions

The **Edwin Smith Surgical Papyrus**, also from the second millennium B.C.E., offers a more systematic approach to medical treatment, focusing on trauma and surgery. Its case-by-case format shows some observational accuracy, particularly in its descriptions of fractures and head injuries. Yet even here, the limitations of Egyptian medicine are evident, especially where magical rituals are prescribed alongside physical treatments.

While this document reveals the presence of some rational procedures, its mixture of magic underscores the **corrupt religious foundation of Egyptian healing arts**, confirming the biblical critique of Egypt's reliance on sorcery rather than on the true God.

### The Brooklyn Papyrus: Evidence of Asiatic Servitude

# THE EGYPTIAN EMPIRE

Among the most significant papyrus finds for biblical studies is the **Brooklyn Papyrus** (c. **18th–17th centuries B.C.E.**), which lists names of slaves in Egyptian households. Notably, many of these names are **Semitic** in origin, providing compelling evidence for the presence of **Asiatic peoples** (including Hebrews) in Egypt during the general time frame associated with the **patriarchal period** and **Israel's sojourn in Egypt**.

The Brooklyn Papyrus does not directly mention Israelites by name, but its record of **foreign servitude** aligns with the biblical assertion that **"a new king who did not know Joseph"** arose and enslaved the Hebrews (Exodus 1:8-14). This indirect confirmation strengthens the historical plausibility of the biblical account, demonstrating that **Semitic populations were present and held as slaves in Egypt** well before the Exodus.

### The Anastasi Papyri: Military, Geography, and Brickmaking

The **Anastasi Papyri**, a series of Egyptian instructional texts from the **Ramesside period (13th century B.C.E.)**, contain details about **Egyptian military campaigns, geography, and brickmaking practices**. These texts mention the use of **straw in brick production**, directly corresponding to the biblical description of the Israelites' labor:

"Let heavier work be laid on the men so that they will keep working and not pay attention to lies… You are no longer to give the people straw to make bricks as before. Let them go and gather straw for themselves." (Exodus 5:9, 7)

The use of straw as a binding agent in mud brick construction is well attested by these papyri, corroborating the biblical narrative's precision regarding labor conditions in Egypt. This evidence rebukes critical attempts to dismiss the Exodus account as fictional or anachronistic, confirming instead that the conditions described are **historically accurate**.

### The Elephantine Papyri: Jewish Presence in Egypt During the Persian Period

The **Elephantine Papyri**, discovered on **Elephantine Island** in southern Egypt, date from the **fifth century B.C.E.** and document the life of a **Jewish military colony** stationed there during the **Persian Empire's rule over Egypt**. These papyri include **legal contracts, marriage documents, letters, and references to the Jewish temple at Elephantine**, which operated alongside pagan Egyptian religious practices.

The existence of this Jewish community aligns with the biblical record of **Jews residing in Egypt after the Babylonian conquest of Judah**, some of whom had fled there against the command of Jehovah through **Jeremiah** (Jeremiah 42–44). Though these documents reflect a post-exilic community, they bear witness to the **continuity of Jewish presence in Egypt** and provide a valuable historical backdrop to later Old Testament events.

Importantly, the Elephantine texts show that these Jews continued to distinguish themselves from the surrounding Egyptians, though sometimes engaging in **compromised religious practices**, including participation in idolatrous customs. This tragic compromise echoes the pattern of earlier Israelite failures to remain distinct from surrounding pagan cultures (compare Exodus 32:1-8).

**The Papyrus Harris: Self-Glorification of Pharaoh and Egyptian Religion**

The **Papyrus Harris I**, a long text from the reign of **Rameses III (c. 1186–1155 B.C.E.)**, offers a royal propaganda piece glorifying the Pharaoh's accomplishments, including donations to temples and military campaigns. While rich in detail, it exemplifies the **self-exalting nature of Egyptian kingship**—a sharp contrast to the **biblical portrayal of Pharaoh as obstinate, idolatrous, and ultimately powerless before Jehovah** (Exodus 5:2; 14:27-28).

The hyperbolic claims of Pharaohs found in such texts highlight the **bias and unreliability of Egyptian historical records**, which systematically avoided any mention of defeat or humiliation. This practice explains the absence of Egyptian inscriptions acknowledging the Exodus plagues or the loss of their army at the Red Sea. Egyptian papyri, with their selective histories, inadvertently validate the **honest** and unembellished nature of the biblical record, which does not shy away from exposing sin—even among God's own people.

### Theological Implications of the Papyrus Discoveries

These valuable papyrus finds, while often arising from pagan contexts, reinforce several key theological points:

1. **The Bible's historical reliability**: The conditions described in the Exodus account, such as slave labor, brickmaking with straw, and Semitic servitude, are consistent with documented Egyptian practices.

2. **The moral corruption of Egyptian society**: The medical, legal, and religious papyri confirm the **superstition, magic, and idolatry** that dominated Egypt—practices condemned repeatedly in Scripture (Deuteronomy 18:9-12).

3. **Jehovah's distinction of His people**: Despite centuries of Israelite presence in Egypt, the biblical record maintains that true deliverance and blessing came not from assimilation into Egyptian culture but through **faithfulness to Jehovah and separation from idolatry**.

4. **Prophetic accuracy**: The failure of Egypt to recover its imperial status, despite periods of cultural activity under Greek and Roman rule, mirrors the long-term judgment foretold by Ezekiel and Jeremiah.

The discovery and study of Egypt's **valuable papyrus finds** provide critical background to the biblical narrative, confirming the accuracy of Scripture in its portrayal of Egyptian culture, economics, religion, and international relationships. These documents, though produced by a people opposed to Jehovah's sovereignty, serve as archaeological witnesses to the truth of His Word.

Their contents validate the biblical depiction of Egypt as a land of **great material achievement but spiritual darkness**, a kingdom humbled by divine judgment and forever incapable of reversing the decree of the living God.

As Psalm 33:11 declares:

"The counsel of Jehovah stands forever, the plans of his heart to all generations."

Thus, even the preserved papyri of Egypt, written by human hands for human glory, ultimately serve the purpose of glorifying **Jehovah, the true God, whose word endures beyond the monuments and scrolls of all empires.**

# CHAPTER 23 What Do the Valuable Papyrus Finds from Egypt Reveal About Biblical Transmission and Historical Reliability?

**Valuable Papyrus Finds**

The discovery of **ancient papyrus manuscripts** in Egypt remains one of the most significant archaeological contributions to biblical studies and Near Eastern history. These finds offer critical insight into the **daily life, administration, religion, and literature of Egypt**, while also providing some of the earliest manuscript evidence for the **transmission of the Holy Scriptures**. These papyri, often preserved for millennia by the **unusually dry and arid climate of Egypt**, would have otherwise perished in the damp conditions typical of most other ancient lands. Their survival not only testifies to Egypt's unique environmental conditions but also to **Jehovah's providence in preserving historical testimony**, both secular and sacred.

While many of these papyri were produced by Egyptians and reflect their idolatrous culture, a number of discoveries directly relate to the **textual history of the Bible**, especially **Old Testament Greek translations and New Testament writings**, strengthening the chain of manuscript evidence that connects modern readers to the original, inspired texts.

**The Preservation Environment of Egypt**

Egypt's climate, characterized by **minimal rainfall and desert sands**, created the perfect conditions for the preservation of **organic writing materials** such as papyrus, leather, and wood. Papyrus, made from the **Cyperus papyrus reed** that thrived along the Nile River, became the primary medium for writing not only in Egypt but also for much of the eastern Mediterranean world until the introduction of parchment (vellum) in later centuries.

In most regions of the ancient world, papyrus manuscripts would have disintegrated within decades due to moisture, insects, and fungi. However, in Egypt, especially in **burial sites, sealed jars, and abandoned settlements**, these documents were often preserved intact for thousands of years. This exceptional preservation has allowed modern scholars to access manuscripts that, in other lands, would have been irretrievably lost.

### Biblical Papyri and the Transmission of Scripture

Among the most valuable finds in Egypt are **biblical papyri**, including early copies of both **Old Testament (Greek Septuagint) texts** and **New Testament writings**. These manuscripts provide crucial evidence for the faithful copying and preservation of the biblical text across generations. Far from being late theological inventions, as liberal critics claim, these ancient papyri confirm that the Scriptures were **widely circulated, copied, and revered** by believers from early on.

### The Chester Beatty Papyri

One of the most significant collections of biblical manuscripts discovered in Egypt is the **Chester Beatty Papyri**, acquired in the 1930s. These papyri, dating from the **second to fourth centuries C.E.**, include substantial portions of:

- The **Pentateuch (Greek Septuagint)**
- The **Gospels and Acts**
- The **Pauline epistles**, including Hebrews
- The **Book of Revelation**

The Chester Beatty Papyri significantly predate the **major vellum codices** like the **Codex Vaticanus** and **Codex Sinaiticus** by over a century. They serve as **vital links between the original autographs of Scripture and the later medieval manuscript traditions**, demonstrating the **early and widespread copying of biblical books**.

These manuscripts affirm that the **content of the New Testament, including its Christological affirmations and apostolic authority, was stable and well-preserved** already in the second century C.E., refuting claims that these doctrines were later inventions.

### The Bodmer Papyri

Another important set of papyri discovered in Egypt is the **Bodmer Papyri**, which also contain early New Testament texts, including:

- Portions of the **Gospel of John** (one of the earliest near-complete copies of this Gospel, dating to around **125-225 C.E.**)
- Sections from **Luke, 1 and 2 Peter, and Jude**
- Portions of Old Testament writings in Greek

The Bodmer Papyri corroborate the **accuracy of the text transmitted through early Christian communities**, further strengthening confidence in the reliability of the biblical manuscripts.

### Papyrus Discoveries and Old Testament Background

Though most biblical papyri found in Egypt pertain to the **Greek Septuagint and New Testament**, the environment has also yielded numerous **Egyptian administrative and legal papyri** that illuminate **the historical background of the Old Testament**. The **Brooklyn Papyrus**, listing **Semitic slaves** in Egypt, supports the biblical claim of **Asiatic servitude during the time frame leading to the Exodus**.

Other non-biblical papyri, such as the **Anastasi texts**, refer to **labor practices, military logistics**, and **geographical knowledge of Canaan and the Sinai Peninsula**, providing cultural context for the **Exodus narrative** and the **Israelite conquest of Canaan**.

These papyri, while not inspired Scripture, confirm that the **biblical descriptions of Egyptian labor, trade, and politics are historically grounded**, not mythological fabrications.

### The Dead Sea Scrolls and Their Connection to Egypt

Though the **Dead Sea Scrolls** themselves were discovered in **Qumran near the Dead Sea**, it is worth noting that **Egyptian papyrus finds complement these discoveries** by filling in manuscript gaps for books that were also found among the Qumran texts.

The textual agreement between the **Egyptian biblical papyri** (such as the Chester Beatty and Bodmer collections) and the **Hebrew texts of the Dead Sea Scrolls** affirms the **remarkable fidelity of biblical transmission across regions and languages**.

This manuscript convergence strengthens the position of the faithful scholar who recognizes that the biblical text, while transmitted by human hands, was **preserved under divine providence with extraordinary care**.

### Papyrus and the Critique of Liberal Theories

The existence of early biblical papyri dating from the **second and third centuries C.E.**, and in some cases even earlier, exposes the **error of Higher Critical theories** that claim the biblical canon was formed late or that core doctrines developed gradually through church politics. The early presence of **complete or near-complete Gospel manuscripts**, the Pauline letters, and the Book of Revelation in these Egyptian papyri demonstrates that **the canon was recognized, revered, and preserved by Christian communities well before the fourth-century church councils**.

These finds confirm that **the text of Scripture did not evolve through mythic accretion or political manipulation**, as critical scholars assert, but was consistently treated as sacred from its earliest copies.

### Papyrus Material and Early Christian Witness

The use of **papyrus codices (book form)** rather than traditional scrolls by early Christians is itself an important historical feature seen in these Egyptian finds. While pagans generally used scrolls, Christians adopted the codex format early, likely for **practical reasons of portability and ease of reference**. This early use of codices among Christian communities reflects their **commitment to wide dissemination of Scripture** and suggests deliberate efforts to **facilitate the spread of the gospel** in contrast to pagan religious systems.

## Conclusion

The **valuable papyrus finds of Egypt**, especially the biblical papyri, serve as **archaeological testimony to the historical reliability and textual integrity of the Scriptures**. They confirm the accuracy of the **biblical description of Egyptian society**, provide **cultural and historical context for Old Testament events**, and validate the **faithful preservation of the Bible's text** through the centuries.

Jehovah's Word has not only been preserved through careful copying by human scribes but also protected through the providential circumstances of history and geography. As Psalm 119:89 declares:

"Forever, O Jehovah, your word is firmly fixed in the heavens."

The papyri of Egypt, though written by mortal hands and stored in fragile materials, serve as enduring witnesses that **the Word of God remains unbroken and true**, unchanged by time, empires, or human opposition.

Edward D. Andrews

# CHAPTER 24 Summary and Theological Reflections on Egypt's Role in Biblical History

Throughout the narrative of Scripture, **Egypt** stands as one of the most prominent foreign nations encountered by the people of Israel. From the earliest chapters of Genesis through the prophetic pronouncements of Jeremiah and Ezekiel, Egypt occupies a complex place in biblical history as both a land of refuge and oppression, a symbol of human pride and false security, and an enduring object of Jehovah's righteous judgments.

Far from being merely incidental to the biblical story, Egypt serves as a key backdrop against which the **sovereignty of Jehovah**, the **faithfulness of His promises**, and the **futility of trusting in human strength** are powerfully displayed. The theological significance of Egypt is not limited to its historical interactions with Israel but extends into the prophetic and eschatological themes of Scripture, where Egypt's role reinforces the central biblical truth that **only Jehovah is God, and His purposes alone will stand** (Isaiah 46:9-10).

### Egypt as a Land of Early Contact with God's People

The biblical account introduces Egypt early in the patriarchal narratives as the place where **Abraham** sought refuge during a famine (Genesis 12:10-20). This initial encounter reveals both Egypt's material prosperity, derived from the **Nile's bounty**, and its moral corruption, as Pharaoh's house is struck by plagues for taking Sarai into his harem. Even at this early stage, Egypt embodies a theme that runs throughout the Scriptures: **a nation rich in earthly resources but bankrupt in spiritual integrity**.

Later, **Joseph's rise to power in Egypt** (Genesis 41) and the subsequent settlement of **Jacob and his family in Goshen** demonstrate Jehovah's providential use of Egypt as a temporary shelter for His people. Yet this period of favor did not endure. The rise of a **new Pharaoh who "did not know Joseph"** (Exodus 1:8) transformed Egypt into the oppressive "house of slavery" (Exodus 13:3), where Israel's identity as Jehovah's chosen nation was forged in suffering and ultimately manifested through miraculous deliverance.

### Egypt as a Symbol of Human Power and Idolatry

Egypt's vast military strength, wealth, advanced culture, and monumental architecture symbolized human achievement at its zenith. Yet, Scripture exposes the **hollowness of these accomplishments when divorced from acknowledgment of the true God**. The ten plagues executed upon Egypt (Exodus 7–12) were not arbitrary displays of power but deliberate acts of judgment "**against all the gods of Egypt**" (Exodus 12:12), revealing their impotence before Jehovah.

Egypt's religious system, rife with **polytheism, animal worship, magic, and necromancy**, epitomized the rebellion of fallen humanity against the Creator. The worship of deities such as **Ra, Osiris, Isis, Horus, and Amon-Ra**, along with the veneration of the Pharaoh as a divine figure, placed Egypt at the center of spiritual opposition to the worship of Jehovah.

The Egyptian magicians, though able to imitate some of Moses' initial miracles through occult practices, were quickly exposed as powerless before the hand of God (Exodus 8:18-19). Pharaoh's repeated hardening of heart (Exodus 7:13; 9:12) became a paradigm of obstinate rebellion against divine authority.

### Egypt as a False Hope for Israel

A central theological lesson throughout Israel's history is the **danger of trusting in Egypt for military or political salvation**. Time and again, the prophets condemned Judah's reliance on Egyptian alliances, warning that help from Egypt was like leaning on a broken reed (Isaiah 36:6). This misplaced trust reflected a deeper spiritual failure—**a refusal to rely on Jehovah alone**.

The prophet Isaiah declared:

"Woe to those who go down to Egypt for help, who rely on horses, who trust in chariots because they are many and in horsemen because they are very mighty, but do not look to the Holy One of Israel or consult Jehovah!" (Isaiah 31:1)

Jeremiah likewise rebuked the remnant of Judah who fled to Egypt after the Babylonian destruction of Jerusalem, against Jehovah's explicit command (Jeremiah 42–44). Their choice to seek refuge in Egypt, even while claiming to worship Jehovah, highlighted their ongoing unfaithfulness. Jehovah's judgment followed them into Egypt, as promised through His prophets.

**Egypt as an Instrument in Jehovah's Judgment on the Nations**

While Egypt often opposed Israel, the Scriptures reveal that **Jehovah also used Egypt at times as an instrument of His judgment upon other nations**, and yet Egypt itself would not escape divine justice. The repeated oracles against Egypt found in **Isaiah 19**, **Jeremiah 46**, and **Ezekiel 29–32** pronounce a comprehensive sentence against Egypt's pride, idolatry, and political arrogance.

Ezekiel's prophecy specifically declared:

"It will become the lowliest of the kingdoms, and it will never again exalt itself above the nations; I will make them so small that they will not rule over the nations." (Ezekiel 29:15)

History has verified this judgment. After its humiliation by Babylon, Egypt was successively dominated by **Persians, Greeks, Romans, Arabs, Ottomans, French, and British powers**, never again achieving the imperial stature of its ancient dynasties. Egypt's political descent stands as a lasting confirmation of the **faithfulness of Jehovah's word**.

**Egypt's Role in the Transmission of Scripture**

Paradoxically, even while under divine judgment, Egypt served as a **preserving ground for biblical manuscripts**, particularly through the survival of **papyrus documents** in its dry climate. The **Chester Beatty** and **Bodmer papyri**, containing some of the earliest known copies of both Old and New Testament texts, were found in Egyptian territories. These finds provide crucial evidence for the **early and accurate transmission of Scripture**, demonstrating Jehovah's providence in maintaining His written revelation even amid foreign lands.

The translation of the Hebrew Scriptures into Greek (the **Septuagint**) during the Ptolemaic period in Egypt further spread knowledge of Jehovah's Word throughout the Hellenistic world, preparing the way for the broader mission of the gospel.

### Egypt in Biblical Typology and Eschatology

While the Historical-Grammatical method rightly rejects speculative allegory and mystical typology, Egypt's role as a **historical symbol of oppression and false trust** is firmly grounded in the inspired text. Egypt stands in Scripture as a perpetual warning against **reliance on human strength, idolatry, and the arrogance of empire**.

Prophetically, the role of Egypt does not end with its historical decline. In the eschatological vision of **Isaiah 19:18-25**, a future is portrayed where Egypt, along with Assyria and Israel, will acknowledge Jehovah and share in His blessings. Yet this picture reflects submission to God's authority, not a restoration of Egypt's political power. Egypt's place in the future is contingent upon **recognizing Jehovah's sovereignty**, not upon its former imperial pride.

### Theological Lessons from Egypt's History

1. **God's Sovereignty Over Nations**: Egypt's rise, power, judgment, and decline are governed not by the whims of human kings but by the deliberate will of Jehovah (Daniel 2:21; Proverbs 21:1).

2. **The Futility of Idolatry and Human Power**: Egypt's strength could not deliver it from the hand of God. Its gods failed, and its armies were powerless before Jehovah's decrees (Exodus 12:12; Jeremiah 46:25).

3. **The Danger of Political Trust Over Spiritual Faithfulness**: Israel's repeated temptation to look to Egypt for help rather than trusting Jehovah remains a timeless lesson for all who would compromise faith for the illusion of security (Isaiah 31:1-3).

4. **The Preservation of God's Word Amid Human History**: Even as Egypt stood judged, Jehovah used its lands to preserve biblical manuscripts that testify to His enduring revelation (Psalm 119:89).

5. **The Certainty of Prophecy**: Egypt's historical trajectory confirms the accuracy and authority of biblical prophecy, reinforcing the believer's confidence that **not one word of Jehovah's promises will fail** (Joshua 23:14).

### Conclusion

Egypt's place in biblical history is a profound testimony to the justice, power, and mercy of Jehovah. It stands as a cautionary example of the **consequences of idolatry and pride** and as a vindication of the prophets who spoke not from their own imagination but from the inspiration of God's Spirit (2 Peter 1:20-21).

Though mighty among men, Egypt was brought low, not by chance or superior human armies, but by the sovereign decree of the One who rules heaven and earth. Its monuments crumble, its dynasties have vanished, but **Jehovah's word endures forever**.

As Psalm 33:10-12 proclaims:

"Jehovah frustrates the counsel of the nations; he nullifies the plans of the peoples. The counsel of Jehovah stands forever, the plans of his heart from generation to generation. Blessed is the nation whose God is Jehovah, the people he has chosen as his own inheritance."

Egypt's story confirms this truth, magnifying the name of Jehovah as the one true God over all the earth.

# Bibliography

Currid, John D. *Ancient Egypt and the Old Testament*. Grand Rapids, MI: Baker Academic, 1997.

Grimal, Nicolas. *A History of Ancient Egypt*. Oxford: Blackwell, 1992.

Hawkes, Jacquetta. *The World of the Past*. New York: Alfred A. Knopf, 1963. (Part V, p. 444)

Hornung, Erik. *History of Ancient Egypt: An Introduction*. Ithaca, NY: Cornell University Press, 1999.

Kitchen, Kenneth A. *On the Reliability of the Old Testament*. Grand Rapids, MI: Eerdmans, 2003.

Kitchen, Kenneth A. *Pharaoh Triumphant: The Life and Times of Ramesses II, King of Egypt*. Warminster, UK: Aris & Phillips, 1983.

Pritchard, James B. (ed.). *The Ancient Near East: Volume I – An Anthology of Texts and Pictures*. Princeton, NJ: Princeton University Press, 1958.

Redford, Donald B. *Egypt, Canaan, and Israel in Ancient Times*. Princeton, NJ: Princeton University Press, 1992.

Shaw, Ian (ed.). *The Oxford History of Ancient Egypt*. Oxford: Oxford University Press, 2000.

Unger, Merrill F. *Archaeology and the Old Testament*. Grand Rapids, MI: Zondervan Publishing House, 1954.

Whiston, William (trans.). *The Works of Josephus: The First Century Jewish Historian*. Peabody, MA: Hendrickson Publishers, 1987.

www.ingramcontent.com/pod-product-compliance
Ingram Content Group UK Ltd.
Pitfield, Milton Keynes, MK11 3LW, UK
UKHW021345220525
6047UKWH00014B/119